Minima Decluttering and Interior Decorating

How to Be a Minimalist Who Lives Intentionally and Organize Your Home and Life Around Things Which are Essential to You and Which Bring You Happiness

By Matt McKinney

© **Copyright 2019 - All rights reserved.**

The content contained within this book may not be reproduced, duplicated or transmitted without direct written permission from the author or the publisher.

Under no circumstances will any blame or legal responsibility be held against the publisher or author for any damages, reparation, or monetary loss due to the information contained within this book. Either directly or indirectly.

Legal Notice:

This book is copyright protected. This book is only for personal use. You cannot amend, distribute, sell, use, quote or paraphrase any part, or the content within this book, without the consent of the author or publisher.

Disclaimer Notice:

Please note the information contained within this document is for educational and entertainment purposes only. All effort has been executed to present accurate, up to date and reliable, complete information. No warranties of any kind are declared or implied. Readers acknowledge that the author is not engaging in the rendering of legal, financial, medical or professional advice. The content within this book has been derived from various sources. Please consult a licensed professional before attempting any techniques outlined in this book.

By reading this document, the reader agrees that under no circumstances is the author responsible for any losses, direct or indirect, which are incurred as a result of the use of information contained within this document, including, but not limited to, —errors, omissions, or inaccuracies.

Contents

Introduction to Minimalism Home 1

Chapter 1: Your Stuff Doesn't Have to be a Burden 5

    Applying Minimalistic Principles to the Design of Your Home............. 7

    Fighting Materialism with Minimalism 9

Chapter 2: How to Start with a Minimalist Lifestyle 12

    If you have read up to this point, then you are aware of why always needing more and hoarding is an issue and how it won't necessarily make a person happy. It is better to start as early as possible in order to implement the necessary changes to life. Below are the steps to getting rid of the clutter and starting with the journey of a minimalist... 12

    Declutter!... 12

    Get Rid of the Boxes 14

    This is simple, but the results are a lot more than simple. Only one benefit of getting rid of the boxes is the fact that future cleaning will be so much easier and so much faster. You should take time to figure out what in your home causes stress and an increase in the noise, even though you may not consider it as clutter. 15

    Manage Your Cables 16

    One In, One Out Rule 16

    Getting Rid of Things 17

Chapter 3: Minimalist Lifestyle is About Freedom 19

Create s Space for Zen 20

Reduce Your Cleaning Time 21

Achieve Financial Freedom 23

Chapter 4: By Choosing to Be a Minimalist, You Will Be More Productive 26

Design Your Home Office 27

Make Sure That Your Electronics Remain Clean and Fast 31

Chapter 5: Create Room for Things Which are Important and Which Deserve It 33

Turn Your Home Into Your Ally 34

How to Resist the Temptation to Buy Unnecessary Clutter 35

Have a List 36

Chapter 6: You are Helping the Environment by Being a Minimalist 38

Achieve Self-sufficiency 38

How to Simplify Your Lifestyle in Order to Benefit the Environment . 40

Chapter 7: By Saving More Money, You Will be Rewarded by Being Able to Buy Nicer Things 42

Create an Amazing Home With Less 43

Always Stay Authentic and Keep Your Creativity Alive 45

Chapter 8: A Large Home Isn't Necessarily a Key to Happiness 48

Minimalistic Living and Budgeting 50

Chapter 9: Stop the Comparison Game 52

    Learn to be Patient 54

Chapter 10: Being a Minimalist Will Make You Happier 56

    How Can You Achieve Happiness Through Minimalism 56

    More Freedom 59

    The Power of Gratitude 59

Conclusion of Minimalism Home 62

Introduction to Declutter and Organize 65

Chapter 1: The Pitfalls of Clutter 67

    What is involved? 69

Chapter 2: You Can Take Action Against The Clutter 71

    Why is Doing This Necessary? 72

Chapter 3: Understand What's Going On 75

    Sign of a Cluttered Life: Angst 76

    Sign of a Cluttered Life: Anxiety 76

    Sign of a Cluttered Life: It's Never Enough 77

    Sign of a Cluttered Life: You are Never Satisfied 79

    Sign of a Cluttered Life: You are Scared You Will Lose Everything 79

    Start by Figuring out What Matters to You 80

Value Audit 81

Do a Detox 82

Chapter 4: How to Start 84

Change You Personal Patterns 86

Just Do It! 88

Don't Forget What is Important 89

Don't Skip Anything 90

Chapter 5: Getting Rid of Mental Clutter 92

The Bottom Line 97

Harmful Emotional Habit # 1: Regularly comparing yourself to other people 99

Harmful Emotional Habit # 2: Drawing Mental Prizes from Material Belongings 101

Harmful Emotional Habit # 3: Immediately Thinking that a Hefty Price Tag Indicates Higher Value 104

Harmful Emotional Habit # 4: Focusing on "Drawing Out" the Benefits People Have Rather Than Viewing Them as Whole People 110

Hazardous Emotional Habit # 5: Freeloading Emotionally Off People 113

Harmful Personality Type # 1: The Black Hole 115

Harmful Personality Type # 2: The Judge 116

Harmful Personality Type # 3: The Stylish Hoarder 117

Toxic Personality Type # 4: The Troll 120

Chapter 6: Getting Rid of Emotional Clutter 124

Look for and Destroy Anti Affirmations 131

How to Create Affirmations That Actually Work as They Should 140

Chapter 7: How to Get Rid of Clutter in Your Career 142

Decide to Love What You Do 143

Discovering the Courage to Let Go 150

Unlocking the Power of Passive Online Income 153

Chapter 8: How to Enjoy More with Less 157

Strip Down the Things You Enjoy 159

Uncovering the Core of Enjoyment 160

Whatever You Do ... Do This 162

Unlocking the Power of Memories 164

Chapter 9: Learn to Be Content 168

Enough is Possible 169

Achieving Emotional Contentment 170

Psychological Contentment 172

Spiritual Contentment 173

Letting Go of Attachments 174

Overcome These Enemies of Personal Change 176

Conclusion of Declutter and Organize 180

Introduction to Interior Decorating on a Budget 184

    Myth Buster 185

Chapter 1: Analyzing Your Home 190

    Common Sense Techniques 191

    The New Home Method 192

    Remodeling an Existing Home 193

    Tips on Setting a Budget 195

    Styles 201

    Tip 205

Chapter 2: Make Small Changes Initially 207

Chapter 3: Taking The Plunge 217

    Goal Setting 218

    Great Goal Setting 219

    Purchasing Products to Decorate Your Home 223

    Painting on a Budget plan 224

    Painting Tips To Save You Money And Time 228

    Total Home Makeovers Extras 232

    Tips for Flooring Improvement 233

Accessorizing Rooms with Hangings, lamps and More 240

Suggestion For Dealing With Clutter 241

The Main Three Changes Everybody Can Make 243

Feng Shui On A Budget 245

Feng Shui and Color On A Budget Plan 246

Prominent Colors 249

Positioning of Objects in the Home 252

Professional Design Tips 256

Decorating for Success 257

Candles Décor 258

Thank you for buying this book and I hope that you will find it useful. If you will want to share your thoughts on this book, you can do so by leaving a review on the Amazon page, it helps me out a lot.

Minimalism

Home

Organize Your Home and Your Life by Practicing Minimalism and Following Practical Strategies for Decluttering and Organizing

By Matt McKinney

Introduction to Minimalism Home

It is way too easy for anyone that is living in today's world to think about never having enough and always needing more in order to achieve happiness. It is easy to spend way too much time and energy imagining having more possessions and stuff in order to alleviate a sense of emptiness inside and absorbing magazines and TV shows and thinking that having more is always the answer.

This envy is only made stronger by various programs on MTV, by countless magazines about interior design and by countless Youtube videos which showcase room after room which all seem to be designed with the sole purpose of stimulating envy and making us eternally unhappy with what we currently have.

When life inevitably gets hard and when we get overwhelmed, it is hard to not think about how better it would all be and how happier we would all be if we had more. Having more always seems like a solution for everything.

To a lot of people, this may sound like truth, but what is ironic is that all of this is false and that the solution for most people would be needing and wanting fewer things and that would actually make them happier. Minimizing a lifestyle is what will enable people to create more space and to actually own more attractive possessions and to enjoy and appreciate the items that are currently in possession of a whole lot more.

You may find this tough to believe, but you already, at this moment, have everything you need in order to create this kind of life and you don't need any extra expense in order to do so. Your family and friends will actually be the ones that are envious when you are done applying what is taught within this book. The home that you own right now can be turned into what you are seeing in media and in order to achieve this, you don't need to buy anything. On the contrary, what you have to do is to get rid of certain things.

After doing this for some time, you will realize that you have actually discovered the way forward by getting rid of the clutter from your life and giving more appreciation toward the things you already own. Doing this will make you into a lot happier person too.

By reading through this book, you can learn how to make these things happen for you and how to make your home so awesome that people visiting your home may think that it is a home of an interior design guru. Doing this may sound expensive, but you will actually be saving a lot of money by doing so. The home that you create this way will support your desired lifestyle and your life will be so much smoother and you will enjoy it a lot more. Along with all the other benefits, your mindset and your perspective will go through a positive transformation that will make happiness so much easier by having a deep appreciation for things that you already have.

By reading through this book, you will learn about how to create your space of zen which will provide you with relaxation that everyone needs. You will also learn how to be more efficient and to make the most out of the things in your vicinity and this is how you will turn your home into a luxurious living space. You will also learn to recognize what is important since that is the only way of decluttering your life and organizing your home and your life. By living like this, you will be saving a lot of money and you will be protecting your environment since you aren't needlessly wasting things.

Your mindset will also take a drastic shift and envy will be a foreign concept for you since you will know how to really appreciate the things which you already own. You will also learn how to create efficient systems which will allow you to reduce the time that would be spent on menial valueless tasks so that you can spend time on what you value the most. By doing this, your level of stress will plummet. You will ultimately learn the true purpose of minimalism and how to incorporate minimalistic principles into your life to transform it for the better.

Chapter 1: Your Stuff Doesn't Have to be a Burden

What does living a minimalist lifestyle mean? Is it more than just another variant of interior design? What is the meaning behind it all? It is about getting everything you ever wanted by realizing you had it all along. Minimalistic life boils down to decluttering and getting rid of non-essentials. It is about reducing your possessions and about the efficiency of doing more with less. Minimalism is a deep appreciation of a couple of things as opposed to a shallow orientation towards many things which you may not even want or care about.

A lot of successful companies such as Apple actually apply minimalistic principles to the design of their products and their devices. Everything has to have a purpose and a reason for being a part of the design and that is why Apple's products aren't overdecorated or overdesigned.

For example, a website design doesn't require complex background or a myriad of menus and it doesn't have to be filled up to the brim with stuff. Everything that is placed on a website should be done so with a purpose and a clear goal and it is necessary to know what wants to be accomplished in order to do this successfully. If the goal is getting the attention of website visitors to a certain element of a website, then the design should accommodate that. It should be clear what is important and what is attempted to be communicated. The button on a website has to have a purpose and the last thing that you want to do is to design a website equivalent of a TV remote.

Applying Minimalistic Principles to the Design of Your Home

These same principles can be applied to the design of your own home although it may not be necessary to communicate something through design or to try to send a profound message.

The furniture which is designed according to minimalistic principles is quite distinct, and when you are looking at such furniture, you can clearly see that there is no unnecessary decoration or a design which doesn't have a reason for being there. Every element of such furniture has a clear purpose and it is all about practicality.

Now that you know how minimalists think about their furniture, now you know what to look for when trying to create a minimalistic home. Now you will be more likely to get rid of the unnecessary stuff and you also won't be tempted to add in more stuff just for the sake of adding stuff. You will also be better at immediately recognizing what is important when a choice is made about furniture.

The reasons why minimalistic design principles have gotten more and more popular are the practicality and improvements of interactions. The minimalistic approach is a more effective design approach since there are fewer distractions and the visitors of a website know precisely what to do and where to go since they are directed to a place where the desired interactions are encouraged. The minimalistic design philosophy when it comes to a website isn't concerned with cramming as many elements as possible since minimalists know that space actually creates calmness and peace. These same principles can be actually applied to the design of your home and by removing what is unnecessary and decluttering, it makes living in your home a lot simpler. By having fewer things and fewer elements, it will be easy and quick to find what you are looking for and hours of life can be saved by doing this over the course of time.

The less clutter there is in a certain place, the less things there are to keep track of and this will provide the eyes with a much-needed rest and restoration. This is what ensures that your home has a sense of peace and calmness and the relaxation and all the other activities will be performed so much smoother.

All this means that you are investing less of your valuable time in mundane tasks such as tidying up and looking for a thing you are trying to find. Your home will be clean and nice to look at most of the time and you will have more time and energy than ever before to dedicate to things that matter to you and that bring you joy.

Similar to UI, your home has a specific role and that role is making sure that your lifestyle is being supported. You need to know if there is a reason for a certain item to be within your home and if there is no good reason you can think of, then that item needs to go. You will breathe so much more easily when your home is designed in this way.

Fighting Materialism with Minimalism

More people than ever are beginning to realize that having fewer things and having fewer possessions can be beneficial. Because of this, people tend to be happier with what they already have and they are less prone to marketing messages which are telling them that they have to buy every single thing that is advertised in order to be fulfilled.

People who focus on less tend to be happier and more satisfied and this is very important since now it is possible to be intrinsically happy since less thought will be given towards thinking about all of the stuff that is lacking.

By adopting this sort of lifestyle, you will also keep your costs down and you will actually have more money to spend on things and experiences that you actually value and which bring you joy. By doing this, you are taking a stance against modern consumeristic culture. This approach is actually quite similar to what many philosophies preached about for a long time. The fact is that happiness comes from gratitude and from appreciating what you do have instead of focusing on what you don't have.

You have probably heard about rich people who seemingly have it all, but are still under stress and are not happy. The reason for that is the fact that they are stretching their budget to the limit in order to support their lifestyle. It can be very easy to get used to a certain way of living and this is especially true if it took a lot of money and a lot of hard work to make that happen. It takes a humongous amount of work in order to make and to maintain such a lifestyle and it can be way too easy to get caught up in the loop of thinking about what a person doesn't have and what is missing.

It is necessary to sometimes stop and to smell the roses and to actually enjoy and appreciate what is there since there is a lot of value and beauty there and it is shame to not notice it and to get lost in the noise. Minimalism can teach you how to get the most out of what you are currently working with and this applies to all areas of life. It is necessary to have a grateful attitude since only then it is possible to appreciate the people and the things around you. Gratitude is what takes happiness to a whole new level when a person realizes the value of the important things such as health and people around them. People that do this are a lot less likely to try to keep up with the Joneses and to always be envious of the grass that is apparently greener on the other side.

Being present is a lot more important instead of mindlessly spending money on things that bring minimal value. Minimalists don't link happiness with what they own and they see their possessions for what they really are. Minimalists enjoy just being able to be with their mind and being able to experience life and they don't let the minor things ruin their whole day.

There are a lot of good things that can be enjoyed in life and they can be enjoyed right now if a choice to do so is made. It is necessary to know how to stop and to appreciate what is here right now instead of always thinking about the next thing or the next fancy toy. People who never have enough are more likely to work more hours and to take loans and those are ultimately short term strategies and what those people have to realize consciously is that they already have everything they need to be happy and that they just need to stop and to reach out and grab it.

By studying the works of great philosophers, it is easy to spot those same conclusions as a recipe for happiness. It is necessary to stop and to appreciate what a person has and by doing this, a lot of stress, dissatisfaction and distractions won't be an issue anymore. This is all easier said than done in a developed world where it seems that every company under the sun is trying to show how awesome their products are and why people can't do without them. However, it is easier with the right knowledge and that is what this book is all about.

Chapter 2: How to Start with a Minimalist Lifestyle

A lot of people throughout the world are living the lifestyle that isn't even close to what is described in this book. There is a good chance that every inch of free space is covered by some clutter and people that live in such homes probably have an extensive list of additional things they want and that they won't think twice about spending their hard earned cash on. There is nothing wrong with wanting the quality of life, but it has to be deserved.

If you have read up to this point, then you are aware of why always needing more and hoarding is an issue and how it won't necessarily make a person happy. It is better to start as early as possible in order to implement the necessary changes to life. Below are the steps to getting rid of the clutter and starting with the journey of a minimalist.

Declutter!

The word clutter was already used enough times in this book, but it is necessary to do so in order to stress how much of an issue it is. It is ok to have nice things, but it is important to know what is actually necessary and what isn't.

You can perform a simple experiment, go into any room in your home right now and go over any surface with your hand. It can be any surface and it doesn't really matter if it's a desk or a chair. Take a look at the items that are currently located on that surface and choose to remove half of them. This may feel unnatural and uncomfortable at first and you will probably manufacture a reason for why you need each one of those things even though you probably haven't used them in years. Still, it is necessary to remove half of them in order to continue with an experiment.

When you are done removing the items which you choose to remove, you will actually realize that the surface looks considerably better, and not just a little better. You are giving space to the items that you actually care about and this way they can stand out more since they do deserve to be able to do so. There is a good chance that you actually couldn't see the surface itself before and that you can see it now since you have eliminated a lot of clutter and this is a lot easier on the eyes and on the mind and it will make you a lot more relaxed.

The items which you decided to keep are the items that are important to you and these items are the better half. By doing this, the average value of the items and possessions that are located on that surface will go up. Now that items may get to chance to be used even more since they will look like they matter instead of just blending into the mess.

What is also neat is the fact that the cleaning will be a lot more bearable since when you have to wipe away the dust from the surface, you will only have to remove a couple of items and you will also have to only put back a couple of items when you are done. The time that will be required for cleaning will be more than cut in half and now you have more time for things that actually matter. Imagine what can be done when you apply this rule to your entire home. To take this experiment to the next level, do the same thing for every surface in a certain room of your choice.

Get Rid of the Boxes

There is a reason why removing clutter is impactful and that is because this is how you can actually get some mental space. Our brains are hard-wired to scan for something to pay attention to and to filter out the things that are worth paying attention to from the things that aren't worth the attention. If it is not easy to realize what is important and what isn't, then the brain will signal the release for more stress hormones. The more clutter and noise there is, the harder the brain has to work to process all that information and this can lead to burnout, especially if a person is tired after a tough day when all a person wants to do is to relax.

More clutter means more work and this is why more isn't always better when it comes to the amount of stuff in our lives and our homes. There are a lot of seemingly innocent items which are causing you stress even if you may not realize that and one example of such items are various boxes that you probably have all around your home. You are probably convinced that boxes are a great item to have since they will make storage that much easier and because they will enable you to get more things out of your way. The reality of the situation is that boxes also can create additional clutter and work.

Boxes will accumulate a lot of dust if they don't have a lid on. What is more important is the fact that boxes are items and items that are not necessary tend to take up space and they occupy your mind. You can perform an experiment by locating all the boxes and taking them somewhere away from your mind's eye. After you have done so, take a moment to notice how clean and how relaxing your home has become. You should search your rooms well for boxes since there is a good chance that they are located in places where it is easy to forget about them, such as under the beds or on top of the shelves.

This is simple, but the results are a lot more than simple. Only one benefit of getting rid of the boxes is the fact that future cleaning will be so much easier and so much faster. You should take time to figure out what in your home causes stress and an increase in the noise, even though you may not consider it as clutter.

Manage Your Cables

Cables are one thing that even people that aren't minimalists get really annoyed with and it is important to manage those cables in some way in order to avoid cable horror. There is a good chance that you have cables in your home which you have completely given up on as far as organization is concerned.

However, these cables do have a potential for creating clutter for the eyes and your home can seem a lot less tidy and organized if they aren't handled properly. Thankfully, there are ways to manage those pesky cables and boxes can be actually used for storing those cables. You can also attach those cables to the underside of the desk and to attach them to the back of the equipment such as monitors. A proper solution for cables will be different for everyone and, therefore, it is necessary to get creative in order to create more space.

One In, One Out Rule

If you want to ensure that your home remains uncluttered, you need to establish certain rules and you need to stick to them. „One in, one out" rule is one rule which you should definitely be sticking to in order to achieve the goal of keeping an uncluttered home. This rule is simple and it consists of getting rid of one item for each new item that you buy and this will make sure that you keep the number of your possessions under control so that you wouldn't fall victim to burnout.

By doing this, you will also be saving money if you make an effort to sell the item that you are getting rid of. In this way you don't have to concern yourself with creating additional space for a new item since every time you buy a new item, a necessary space is created. Practicing this rule will force you to really think about which things are important to you and worth keeping.

This rule could sound a bit extreme, but you should just try it out and once you see the results, then there won't be a doubt in your mind about this rule being the right thing to follow.

Getting Rid of Things

Just by implementing these tips, you will realize that you are getting rid of a surprising number of things. It is necessary to mention again that this process isn't easy. Change is not easy for most people.

In order to start, you should start with a bang and you should do a large declutter where you quickly get rid of a lot of stuff. This is a good way to reset your home and your life and it gives you a fresh start. This is really powerful since people love the sense of a new beginning and a new adventure.

The first step to decluttering is filling up the boxes with things that have been sitting in the storage for too long and that will likely not be used again. If something hasn't been used in 6 months or more, then it should go in the box. The things that hold sentimental value or which are very monetarily valuable are an exception to this rule, however.

The crucial tip to getting rid of things is to do it quickly since you may hesitate and quick altogether if you stop and think for too long. Before you start discarding, you should see if any of the items could be sold for a decent price, and if they can, then you want to keep those so that you can sell them as soon as possible. Everything that is left can either be donated to a charity or thrown out for good.

As far as selling items is concerned, don't try to sell each item since going through each item and evaluating it will create additional stress and this only increases the chances of abandoning the whole process.

Chapter 3: Minimalist Lifestyle is About Freedom

If you are still not sure if minimalism is a good choice, then just think of how hard it will be to move with a lot of possessions. Moving and changing homes with a lot of clutter and a lot of stuff isn't fun and this is the situation where all the stuff that you don't need will come to bite you in the butt.

The goal is to reduce the things which you own to the essentials which you can't do without and to things that you love and which are meaningful to you. When you do that, moving will be exponentially easier and faster. Moving is not easy and it is not necessary to make it even tougher.

Doing this also gives you an option of putting all your belongings in a backpack and traveling the world at your own leisure. The world is your oyster when you can do this. You can also rent out your home as you travel in order to truly be efficient.

This is one example of how having less clutter actually provides you with freedom. Traveling the world in this way simply wouldn't be nearly as possible if you had a lot of stuff weighing you down. You simply can't be as flexible when you have a lot of stuff and it is, pretty much, akin to being anchored. I can promise you that you will feel light as a feather when you have less mess in your life weighing you down.

Create s Space for Zen

There are a lot of ways in which having less stuff can be liberating and one more example of that is the fact that less stuff means less stress. It can be said that a home is a reflection of the owner's mindset. Life will get busy for anyone at certain times and the home can be a reflection of a situation when it feels like the weight of the world is on top of the owner. It can be easy for clutter to accumulate all around and it can seem impossible to get around to actually managing that clutter.

The sink may be full of dishes or the papers could be lying around and it can be very hard to relax in such circumstances, and even when a time for relaxing does come, it is hard to actually get the most out of that relaxation since the messiness of the home acts as a reminder of all the issues.

When the home is messy, there is always a lingering feeling about chores having to be done. This makes it additionally harder to relax properly and to put your mind at ease.

Even if you are doing everything very well as far as being a minimalist is concerned, there will still be situations in which not everything is as it should be and these situations will inevitably cause you to get stressed since things are not happening according to your expectations. In order to combat this, you should create your space of Zen and this will be any place or a room within your home where there will never be any mess. Design in that room will be even more minimalistic and that will be accomplished with the addition of even more rules such as no food or drinks being allowed inside or not being allowed to enter wearing shoes.

The goal of having such a place within your house that will always be neat and organized no matter what happens is to make sure that you always have a place where you will be able to just sit down and to shut off the rest of the world while you do some unwinding activity such as reading a book.

Reduce Your Cleaning Time

As mentioned earlier, you will be spending a lot less time cleaning up when you live like a minimalist and this will additionally minimize the amount of mundane work that is necessary to keep things as they should be since you are using efficient systems.

It is a fact that most people spend more time than they would like performing tasks that aren't really engaging but have to be done such as doing the laundry or dishwashing or ironing the clothes or any other chore. These activities can take away the time which you could be spending on fulfilling activities such as spending time with people that matter to you, or doing something important such as writing a book.

A lot of tedious parts of life will be reduced by becoming a minimalist and doing something as simple as having fewer possessions will drastically reduce the time which you would otherwise have spent cleaning up. The same principles could be applied to any other possession you may have and this will also contribute to reducing the time spent doing chores so that same time could be put into something you value.

If you want to take all of this a step further, you should have systems in place which will ensure that the work goes a lot more smoothly. For example, investing upfront into a dishwasher could eliminate the chore of having to manually clean the dishes and while the whole chore of dish cleaning is being done by the machine, you can do something else like dealing with some other chore. Dishwashers cost money upfront, but they will save you time, and you have to realize a lot of choices in life boil down to a tradeoff between time and money.

You can create systems for a lot of other things such as paperwork so that you could organize them in as little time as possible. You can also make a plan for the clothes that you will wear so that you have to make fewer decisions which will make sure that you avoid decision fatigue. There is a reason why a lot of successful people use this life hack.

You have, without a doubt, seen one of those robotic vacuum cleaners and investing in one of those is also smart if you really want to cut down on the time spent vacuuming.

To summarise the point of all these examples, minimalism isn't just about how things look, it is also about making sure that a certain place requires minimal upkeeping and maintenance which no one really likes to do and this can even include choosing foods which take less time to prepare even though they may not taste as good as some other options which would require longer preparation time.

Achieve Financial Freedom

Maybe the most important thing about being a minimalist is the fact that you can buy yourself a good chunk of financial freedom since you have fewer requirements and fewer things which you just have to have. This means that your expenses are significantly lower and the amount of money you need in order to achieve happiness is a lot lower. This will make your life a lot easier and a lot more enjoyable since you won't be so financially worried since you won't have as much debt which would have to force you to do the things which you don't want to do.

The wealth isn't only about how much money you bring in; it is about the difference between the money you bring in and the money you spend. Obviously, by reducing the amount of money that you spend, your wealth will go way up and that is what will give you options in life.

After reading through this chapter, it should be clear to you how you don't need to accumulate stuff in your life in order to be fulfilled and to make your home a pleasant place to live in. Even though that not buying countless unnecessary things is a piece of good advice, it is still advisable to sell things which you don't have a use for anymore and this will be really helpful as far as saving cash is concerned. If you are reading this, there is a good chance that you are a smartphone user, and if you care about always having the latest model, then you can trade in your current model for the latest one when the time comes and you will be able to get the latest model with minimal cost when the time comes.

In the same way, you can also save a lot of money by using what you already have and being resourceful instead of constantly buying new things. In order to implement this, you should know ahead of time what you like doing in order to be able to do what you want. As a result, you can focus more of your time and energy on meaningful things such as reading books.

If there is some way to make your life more simple by still keeping things and activities you care about, then do so. By applying what is described in this chapter, you will save loads of money over the long term and you will be able to live without a worry knowing that you don't have to worry about debt or wondering if you can actually afford something that would make you happy. This carefree kind of living will make sure that you are so much more comfortable than what you would be by having a lot of stuff.

Your whole life can be designed by using the principles I just outlined and by adopting this kind of thinking, you will automatically consider getting a smaller house instead of a larger one if that means that your mortgage installments will be lower which will ensure that you keep more money and therefore more freedom.

Chapter 4: By Choosing to Be a Minimalist, You Will Be More Productive

Have you ever thought about how many things which you own you don't even use or don't even know the purpose of? Does this realization make you more stressed?

Now let's imagine the opposite situation: You are completely aware of all of your possessions and you can very quickly remember all the things that you own and the reason for owning those things. Doesn't this second situation feel so much better? This approach will actually provide you with a lot more energy and a lot less stress and your productivity will skyrocket as a result. This may be subtle, but the chances are high that the mess and the lack of organization in your home impact your productivity in a negative way.

If you want to be able to do good work, then you have to make sure that you intentionally design your working space. This doesn't have to be complicated since complexity is the enemy of execution. For example, when your home is more pleasant, then you will be more likely to stick to your hygienic habits and your other healthy habits that have to get done.

When you have to search every corner and every drawer to find what you want, that adds up over the course of days and weeks and you can lose a lot of your time and energy which will ensure that your life will take a hit. This chapter is all about showing you how being more minimalistic can improve your productivity with your work and all areas of life.

Design Your Home Office

When most people think about being productive at home, they will think of something like a personal office within their homes where they keep all necessary things for doing the work such as a computer or relevant files and all the other items that may be helpful. It is necessary to plan and to know what may be necessary for the work so that you don't get interrupted by having to look for things that aren't within the reach of your hand.

If you are fortunate enough to have a career which allows you to work from home, or if you just like to have space within your home where you do your administrative duties, then this chapter will prove to be quite helpful.

For the most people, this office space within a home will not be very tidy and organized and it will look like a bomb went off when you see all the papers and tools and cables lying around.

In order to get this organized, you need to make sure that you have a system for organizing your documents. The good old filing cabinet will do the trick here. You do have to know which documents are actually appropriate for filling since there are some documents which you may need to use more frequently. You can achieve this kind of organization by using paper trays and you should use those while keeping how human memory works in mind.

You should have one tray which is used for all the current projects which are handled right at the moment of working. This tray should be dealt with every day and it is necessary to get rid of things that shouldn't be there anymore by either getting rid of them or putting them on another tray.

At the end of the work week, which will most likely be Friday, you will take anything that is still left on the current tray and you will place it in the filing cabinet if you deem it important enough while throwing away anything else that is considered unimportant. This is effective because it is acknowledged that there are some things that may require quick access and recovery. Also, by sticking to this system over the course of time, you make sure that the paperwork doesn't pile up and that it is put where it won't be able to create a mess.

If you can, then you should make an effort to reduce the quantity of paper you are working with. You should always have some kind of notepad with you so that you could capture ideas before they disappear and you should always think if converting a certain document to a digital format makes sense and you should do so if you determine that digitalization is the best choice.

By doing this, the organization will be so much easier. It is also a good idea to invest in a scanner which you can use to scan important documents so that you could convert them into a file that will be possible to work with on a computer. If you think that a physical form of the scanned document is no longer necessary, then you can simply get rid of it.

If you implement these changes into your system, the work which is required for paperwork all around your home will be much easier to manage and that will ensure that your home makes it easier for you to be productive.

Again, knowing how to manage your cables is pretty important. If it is possible to use a wireless variant for certain electronics, then you should do so since it will make your life so much easier. If you are really serious about this, then you can purchase a product such as Amazon Echo which will allow you to issue voice commands to your computer.

In order to be more productive, it is all about making the procedures simpler and removing the obstacles and doing this fairly regularly. The fewer steps there are to completing a certain task, the more efficient a system is. Everything that you may require to do your work should be within your reach and this is a variant of French cooking concept known as mise en place. Designing your home like this will save you hours.

The goal of removing clutter and obstacles is to make getting the work done easier and smoother. If a certain item or a certain piece of furniture doesn't serve a purpose within your office, then you should get rid of it from your office to make things easier for you. Any extra items that are in your office have the potential to be a distraction and that is why you should carefully consider what is in your office and what isn't. You want to make a separation between your working life and your personal life and doing this actually resets your brain.

The place in which the work is done shouldn't be used to do fun things and that is why a bookshelf or a TV has no reason for being there since that will only put ideas of fun in your head. The room in which you do your work shouldn't necessarily be bland and it is actually a good idea to add some color to that room if that will help your productivity. When choosing a color, remember that certain colors are better for productivity instead of others and light green, for example, is relaxing since it is similar to what you would see when looking at plants and that simply feels good.

The point is that if you don't like corporate looking environments, then you shouldn't design your working space as one. Just make sure that the room in which you do work doesn't have things which have the potential to distract you and this will make procrastination a whole lot harder. Using each line of defense against procrastination is necessary.

Make Sure That Your Electronics Remain Clean and Fast

It is important for a piece of technology to keep doing its job well and without hiccups. Just as you want to make sure that the room in which you are doing your work is nice and tidy and without clutter, you want to apply the same logic and the same rules to the computer you are working on. If the desktop of your computer is covered with icons that you don't use, then that is also an issue for productivity since that will stress you out. That could also slow down your computer and that will also cause a lot of stress which will ruin your productivity plans.

You want to take the organization of your files seriously since you don't want for important files to go missing. You also don't want for your computer to be too slow since that will make you anxious each and every time you boot up your computer. The minimalistic design principles are not limited to only your room and you should be applying them to the design of your computer as well. If there is an unnecessary file, then you want , and you also want to make sure that your antivirus software is a good one. You also want to know if there is a good reason for installing a particular piece of software. It is extremely satisfying when your computer is running as it should and when you are not being taken out of the flow of the work by a slow computer.

Chapter 5: Create Room for Things Which are Important and Which Deserve It

In order to be successful with the implementation of minimalistic principles, it is necessary to really think about what you want to achieve in your life and what kind of home design has to be achieved to make sure that your goals are achieved.

You don't want to be in a situation where your home is an obstacle to working toward your goals and to working effectively and efficiently. It should be the opposite, your home is what should make things easier for you so that you have a better chance of accomplishing what you want.

The question you may be asking now is why does it happen that so many people don't utilize this philosophy of home and life design? The answer to that is actually quite simple and it boils down to the fact that some people simply don't know what they want from their home and from life as a whole. One thing that could be blamed for all this is media and marketing since they are constantly showing us a supposedly better way to live which is better than what we are currently doing. This makes it hard to be satisfied and to know what you actually want. As a consequence, it is easy to get lost in a sea of different marketing agendas and goals. It is really hard to be truly happy when we are constantly hearing about a better way to do something.

In order to not fall for anything, you need to stand for something. You need to sit down and to really think about what is important to you and what you want to get out of life since you can't get what you want if you don't know what you want. You should write down an affirmation based on what you want and you can start to build your ideal home by using that as a guide. The point is that you don't want to be without the knowledge of what goals are important and the strategies for moving towards those goals.

Turn Your Home Into Your Ally

Maybe you came to the realization that what you really value the most in your life are the people close to your and music. Now that you have this knowledge, you can start designing your Home appropriately. For example, you may design your home in a way that accommodates guests so that they want to spend more time there. The rooms which would go a long way towards accomplishing these design goals would be some form of entertainment rooms such as rooms with comfy furniture and a large television accompanied with a large table for all the snacks. As far as the love of music is concerned, you could design a room completely for that and select the most appropriate decorations.

In both of these examples, you are making a decision about the design based on your whether or not a certain purchase will get you closer or further from what you are trying to achieve. You are also considering if a certain decision will bring joy or not. You also begin to include more dimensions into your decision-making process such as an opportunity cost and whether a purchase of something is an objective improvement.

When you think like this, then it will be much harder for you to be influenced by marketing campaigns since you clearly know what you want and you won't be satisfied until you are successful in achieving that. That is easier said than done however and there are still certain urges to resist.

How to Resist the Temptation to Buy Unnecessary Clutter

When you are considering making a purchasing decision, you should have a checklist you want to run through in order to determine if a certain purchase will improve your lifestyle. Think about the long term implications of the purchasing decision.

It is also very helpful if you are educated about all the small subtle tricks which marketers tend to use in order for people to spend their money on something for which they didn't even know they wanted. When you are about to buy something, you want to use that as a trigger to slow down and to think through your decision. Most of the purchases are made emotionally and by slowing down, you can protect yourself from being too impulsive for your own good. The solution in this situation is to think logically and rationally about what you really need for your situation and by doing this over a course of time, you will be surprised at the improved quality of your decisions.

If you are going to buy something, then have a plan for the purchase beforehand and by doing so, you will not be making purchases on the spot. Whatever you were thinking about buying will likely be there and if you determine that that same thing is actually valuable, then you can go ahead with the purchase.

Have a List

There is a way to resist the temptation of buying new shiny stuff, and that is having a list of things that you really want to do. You may think that this is redundant and that you can easily keep track of everything, but the fact is that people are forgetful and that there are a lot of things that tend to get left unattended such as books that were never read or recipes that were never tried out or various activities that never seem to get their turn to be tried out. These activities can be anything from learning a new language to catching up with an old friend.

It can be easy to forget about all these things when some free time finally becomes a reality and then it can be easy to follow the path of least resistance and to simply slump in front of the TV.

It really may not be necessary to buy a new book when there are so many other books that are waiting to be read. Instead of working away in order to save money for a new TV, it can be good to remind yourself of the joy of simply going to a park or to a newly opened museum. Having a list where your ideas for an evening are listed is a really useful strategy. You can turn to that list every time you get the urge to buy something and by doing this, you will come to the realization that there are plenty of options already in your vicinity which don't require spending money, or at least not as much. You should look at your home as an ally on your path to your goals.

Chapter 6: You are Helping the Environment by Being a Minimalist

Being a minimalist doesn't just have to be about yourself and it doesn't just have to be about you wanting to make your home look better. Being a minimalist is actually good for our planet and there are many examples which can make this evident.

Take a moment to think about all the fancy gadgets which you have with yourself at all times. If you are living more like a minimalist, that means that you aren't spending that much time in front of a TV and this will reduce your costs since you won't have to pay as much for an electrical bill and the maintenance of your home as a whole.

Achieve Self-sufficiency

If there is one thing that minimalists strive for, then that goal is self-sufficiency. Minimalists need less to be happy, and therefore, happiness is much easier to achieve. A simpler life implies that you, by yourself can fulfill your needs and that way, you are freeing yourself from having to work longer hours in order to achieve a more costly lifestyle.

There are several ways to turn self-sufficiency into reality and one of those ways is to have your own garden where you will be growing your own fruits and veggies. This will provide you with what you need for health and you will also not have to spend so much at the supermarket. Doing this is also good for the environment since you are minimizing the greenhouse gas issue be creating your own ecosystem.

Another avenue of achieving self-sufficiency is by taking control of your own power and electricity. This is much easier by being a minimalist since that means that less power is required in order to keep the minimalist lifestyle up and running smoothly. Taking care of your own power is also good for the environment since you are actively reducing carbon emissions. The one mainstream option of making this work is by installing solar panels, but it is necessary to know that this option is pricey and that a lot of work is involved in getting solar panels up and running and it may require a lot of patience and waiting before seeing a return on investment.

In order to really start generating some power, you should get yourself a solar generator and you can even purchase a portable version of the solar generator. This is very important if you want to travel around since it will allow you to carry it with yourself. You will have to spare of a couple of thousands of dollars for this, although it is still a good investment and you might also get some solar panels as part of the package. All this will ensure that you have enough electricity to run your most essential electronic devices such as computers and fridges as long as nothing happens to the generator.

The generator does cost some money, but it still a better option than renovations which would also be costly.

Another trick you could use is to collect water from the rain and using some items which you can find around the house as long as they can provide you with usefulness. This is how you help yourself by reducing your spending. You will also be helping the environment since you will be wasting a lot fewer things.

How to Simplify Your Lifestyle in Order to Benefit the Environment

There are various methods which you can use to downgrade your lifestyle to the essentials which will ultimately benefit the environment. You can use your car less often since you will be saving money on fuel and you will be reducing carbon emissions. It will be pretty good for your health if you walk to places or use a bike.

In order to reduce costs further and to improve your health and the environment, you can cut down on the red meat. Red meat is pricey, but it can also be bad for the environment if it is wasted.

You can also go green and by doing this, you are giving priority to products that are made in a way that is efficient and good for the environment. If you want to signal what changes you want to see, then vote with your wallet and support green organizations. If you choose to do so, then you will get rid of a lot of clutter from your life since there will be a lot of items which you will no longer be using.

Chapter 7: By Saving More Money, You Will be Rewarded by Being Able to Buy Nicer Things

We have covered a lot of steps and tactics which can be used to edit a lifestyle and to make it more minimal with the freedom as the ultimate goal. If you have read up to this point, you have probably already thought of some ways you can apply some of these things to your situation.

It is necessary to point out that it isn't about scaling down so much that you are left with nothing. It is all about putting yourself in a position which will allow you to live life as you want it and on your terms. This isn't accomplished by getting more stuff, but rather by being resourceful and using what you already have. This is a lot safer way of getting to freedom.

In order to save money successfully, it is necessary to know what you actually want so that you wouldn't be spending automatically and unconsciously. It is not just about doing less, but about doing less and better instead of doing a million things shallowly.

A simple act of clearing the surface of things can be powerful. Imagine the added benefit of putting the things that make you happy on those surfaces. The difference is significant and noticeable in an instant. By doing small simple things such as these, you can create a pretty luxurious home.

Create an Amazing Home With Less

In order to get the home as you see in magazines, you really don't have to spend that much money. Before you start, you need to know exactly what kind of home you want and by doing this, you will be able to make a lot quicker decisions about the furniture you want.

There are actually only a couple of key features on which you want to focus on when designing a home if you want to leave a lasting impression on guests and visitors. You need to know how to select items that will complement your whole home and which will fit in well. You want to choose these things carefully since you are representing yourself through them.

For example, a neat design choice for your bathroom is to set up entry into a shower to look like when a person is entering a waterfall. Doing this can change the feel of the whole room in a good way and this will increase the level of comfort. You can also add a fireplace to your living room and this will make it a lot more comfortable to be in and it will make it more memorable.

The choice about this is completely yours and you don't want to be shy about your choices since this will only be successful as long as you are authentic. It is possible to have a pool in the garden or a chandelier, but you can only add those successfully if your design is minimal and if nonessential things are cut out. You have to know what kind of lifestyle you really want and then you want to design your home around that since that is the only way you can make things described in this chapter possible. You need to think long and hard about your priorities.

A lot of people that visit your home may leave full of envy, but the funny thing is that you may be spending less money than them. The key elements of your home really come in sharp focus when you actually remove the clutter and non-essentials which are just a distraction. This is accomplished by spending less instead of spending more.

This kind of success can be linked back to having a clear vision and knowing what you want so that you can work towards it and design your life and your living space around that. Once you know what you want, then you also know what you don't want and that is how you start cutting things out.

Always Stay Authentic and Keep Your Creativity Alive

There are a lot of opportunities to be unique and being unique and taking a stand for something means more than trying to fix an issue by throwing more money at it. Your guests will remember the visit to your place more if you show them something that is new to them. You can only do this successfully if you stay true to yourself and if you don't compromise before you achieve what you want.

You may be into working out and you could design your home around that by having your home gym, but if you really want to stand out, then you can extravagantly decorate your gym equipment and this will impress anyone that walks in. This won't cost much and it will be quite original and memorable. Anyone who sees gym like this may end up leaving full of envy since working out may seem quite fun there and that would make working out regularly so much easier.

If you want to succeed in life, you do need some creativity. You really want to think about what message you want to send through the design of your home and what idea would be behind it. You want to be keenly aware of why some things will always have a place in your home.

By thinking about this, you may come up with some alternatives which will really save you money. Maybe you have always wanted to have one of those wardrobes into which you simply walk in, but you don't have that wardrobe yet because you find it too draining on your budget. You want to really think why you want that wardrobe and what is the main reason because of which you want it. You may conclude that you just love fashion and that you love to display your good taste for everyone to see in a stylish manner.

It is great that you know why you want something, but you can achieve that same goal without necessarily buying this kind of wardrobe by being a little creative which may lead to the discovery of even better and fancier solutions than what you first envisioned.

If you buy a bookshelf, which is a lot cheaper, you could use it to display your shoes and other clothing items instead of books. In order to save even more money, you could also select a wall within your home and decorate it with shelves exclusively for your fashion.

By doing this, you will still be impressing your visitors and you will be doing it for a fraction of a price and that is a prime example of creativity and resourcefulness. Now that you have saved some money, now you can buy nice things for yourself and you can focus on your lifestyle and the things that matter to you.

Chapter 8: A Large Home Isn't Necessarily a Key to Happiness

Everyone needs to make a decision for themselves concerning how minimal they want to go and it is necessary to set some kind of boundary. Is it your goal to scale back to the fullest and to live in the wilds without any technology? Do you want to create an amazing lifestyle by using only a couple of items which will make your home look very luxurious even though it doesn't require much maintenance and upkeeping?

You need to anticipate your expenses before you make the decision. Every minimalist will have a different vision in mind when designing a lifestyle and for some, it may be about traveling while for others it may be about being financially abundant and having the option of sending kids to college stress-free.

For example, if you are someone who lives to travel, then it's quite obvious why buying a large house may not be the best choice for you. All that you need in order to achieve the lifestyle of travel is to get yourself a one-room apartment in an area which you can afford. By doing this, you have more money to do your favorite thing, which is traveling. When you live in a small home, then your minimalist capabilities will be really tested and you will really have to make some tough choices about what is important to you so that you could make the whole situation work in your favor.

Doing all these things and living like this is what the marketing industry doesn't want you to find out since people like that separate from their money less easily. As mentioned before, modern life is great, but it also attempts to manufacture demand for the things which people never wanted in the first place. It is intended to give people a boost of motivation so that they would work harder and earn more money for the corporations.

What you really do need in life is to take care of your health and to have a cozy place to stay at. If you spend some time searching and exploring, you may discover a property which is the ideal size for your needs and even if you take out a mortgage for such a property, you can pay it off in its entirety in a couple of years. You just need to be disciplined in a combination with principles of being a minimalist in order to get the things which you want and which you need to be happy for as little money as possible all in a couple of years.

The goal is to never have to worry about debt again and to find more ways to generate income so that you can quit the 9 to 5 rat race. It is possible if you want it and if you don't stop working until you get it.

Minimalistic Living and Budgeting

As it was mentioned enough times already, you need to clearly know what you want since that is the only way of you knowing what to do and which steps to take. When you have a plan, then you can take action in order to make that plan into a reality.

You need to have a budget if you want to reach your goals. This budget doesn't have to be complicated and all that you have to do is to include all your income and all your expenses and all of this you should put into an excel spreadsheet and you should do so regularly. Doing this over a course of time will give you a clear picture of your financial situation and you will be able to see if your finances are going up or down.

At the end of a certain period of time such as a week or a month, you will be able to see how much money is left and you can choose to either spend this money however you want it or you can save it.

In order to actually manage to remain consistent with this, you have to keep reminding yourself why you are doing what you are doing and you need to keep reminding yourself of your vision. Whatever your goal is, you want to know how much will your path towards your goal cost you and based on that, you could get an idea of how much time it should take you to reach a goal.

Now that you have an approximation of how much time you will need in order to reach your goal, you need to try to cut that time down and to shorten it. You can do so by reducing your costs on things which you don't actually need. You can also sell some items which you aren't even using. One more option is to reduce some other costs by eating out less or buying less things that aren't really necessary. You can also look at the list of fun and cheap activities which you have compiled before in order to keep your costs down. Just taking a walk could be so much better instead of spending an evening watching Netflix and your wallet will also love it.

Over the course of time of doing this, being more minimal will become second nature to you. The key tip for staying on track is reminding yourself of your reason for doing what you are doing. The end result of all of this is having more time and energy which you can give to the people that matter the most to you, such as your family and your friends.

Chapter 9: Stop the Comparison Game

It can be quite easy to make visitors of your home envious if you design it as it was described. There is a good reason for trying to impress visitors of the home and that is because that is what drives the purchasing decisions for most people even if they don' want to admit it. It is simply encoded into humans to be aware of their standing in the relation to other people and to always try to look at the side of their neighbors thinking the grass is greener on the other side.

Actually using the driving force of caring about what people think can be used to increase productivity and it can help them to achieve great things which could go a long way as far as increasing status is concerned. Being the leader of the pack was a huge driving force back in the day, but today it can actually lead to decreased happiness if that drive isn't controlled.

I know it may sound ridiculous, but this has been proven by psychological studies and the name of this theory is „social comparison theory" which basically states that comparison to others can have a huge impact on how happy we feel and how accomplished we feel.

One study focused on determining how happy people who earn different salaries are. It was discovered that the absolute amount of money earned didn't matter all that much. What does matter to people is how much are they earning in comparison to other people in their circle.

For example, you could be earning 150 000$ a month which is great money, but it would still be harder to be happy when you are aware at all times that other people in your circle are earning twice that amount. This kind of comparison can make you less satisfied even though you can do almost anything with that kind of money.

On the other hand, if your earnings were around 1000$ a month while everyone else was earning half of that, then you would actually feel a lot happier and accomplished. Social comparison is real and there is a good chance that it is behind a lot of wrongdoings and depression. It is a fact that a lot of people struggle with this.

It gets even worse. Before people were only comparing themselves with people in their local circle and with whom they associate daily. But today, with the world being more connected, it can seem like the whole world is one big city and now people will compare themselves to the celebrities too which may not even be on the same side of the globe. It is harder to be happy when you are constantly seeing how much fun everyone else is having on social media.

The solution is quite simple and it is to stop comparing your life to others and to snap out of it. Stop constantly trying to get the things which others have and start showing appreciation towards the things which you own already. This is easier said than done, but you really have to think about what you want and what is important to you in your life.

By doing this, it will be a lot harder to keep comparing yourself to others since you will realize that you value different things and that things which make other people happy won't necessarily make you happy. You may think you want something, but it may not improve your life in any way and it might just end up being a burden which will require maintenance which will make being happy harder.

It may take some time to rewire your mind, but eventually, you can realize that it is not important what your neighbor has since thinking like that will lead to better decision making and more happiness and fulfillment in life. You will know what is important to you and what is worth your money and that is how you make your life better and something worth being happy about.

Learn to be Patient

There is another mental shift which you need to make and that is to train your patience. Being able to delay gratification and to be patient can protect you from a lot of bad choices since you won't be getting in debt and spending money which you don't have on clutter just because you want it right now.

There is bound to be a lof rationalizing in favor of buying things right at that moment such as thinking that a certain item will be gone for good if it isn't bought right now. The main issue is in the buying habit since buying something before you can afford it means that you are likely to buy another item, in the same manner, the next week as well.

You need the discipline to be successful in life and you need to know what you want so that you would be aware of what you can and what you can't do. Doing this will ensure that your life is a lot less stressful and a lot less filled with debt which will make sure that your home is more likely to stay clean and free of clutter. You need discipline if you want to keep your life under control and in balance.

Chapter 10: Being a Minimalist Will Make You Happier

Through the course of this book, you have seen how being more minimal can allow you to have more savings, improve the environment, make your home a lot more dazzling to anyone who visits and ultimately helping you get out of the rat race so that you can live on your terms and do what you want.

All these causes are worth fighting for. Changing your thinking and decluttering your home is a good start for anyone who wants to be more fulfilled in life. Those all things are nice, but what it is ultimately about is being happy and loving life. That is possible when you decide to scale down and become minimal.

How Can You Achieve Happiness Through Minimalism

Minimalism can make people happier in two ways. Minimalism can cause a complete shift in perspective and in how people look at their possessions. This chapter is all about explaining how being minimalistic can lead to more happiness.

To recap, living a minimal lifestyle will enable you to have more time. Since your home is less cluttered, that also means that there is less cleaning up to do. If you have taken the time to figure out and to implement systems and processes so that your house could be kept clean in a way that minimizes the required maintenance.

When you are living in this way, it is so much easier to just unwind and to relax when you finally come home. It is hard to put in words how impactful it is having a simple home and it is something that needs to be experienced firsthand in order to comprehend it.

Living like a minimalist will reduce your stress. Since your lifestyle doesn't require as much money expenditure, you don't have to work as much. It is quite a realization when you figure out that you don't need to do overtime in order to get the things which you want. You will then look at so many people who trade hour after hour and wonder why someone traps themselves in such a way of life. You can be happy without needing to work more.

When you live like this, you are coming home a whole lot earlier and you are a lot more relaxed and fun to be around since you are not carrying the stress with you. There are some people that actually derive satisfaction and purpose from their work and they may be hesitant to live like this because of that, but it doesn't have to be that way and there are plenty of ways to get fulfillment from other things that aren't work. When you live like this, you can just ditch everything and go traveling to Asia for three months without having to ask anyone.

You also have an opportunity to try out something entrepreneurial and to try to figure out how to make money online. Since you have fewer things that you have to attend to around the house and because of that, you will be less pressured to go after money at the expense of other areas of life. You can only be out of balance for so long.

If something does go wrong, which it inevitably does, you aren't short on savings which you can use to make a problem, such as a boiler issue, go away by merely paying a mechanic so that he could come to fix it. When you have extra money saved, you can use it to make most problems go away and things like a car breaking down become just an annoyance instead of financial stress.

If you don't have any debt, then you don't have to worry if you will be able to cover your next installment and the life is just more fun when you don't have to worry about as many things and when you can focus on living presently and in the moment.

More Freedom

You are freer when you don't have to worry about all the things you have to maintain in order to make it through life. The interesting thing is that you don't need to concern yourself with your house being robbed while you're not at home since you don't have many things with you at one time in the first place.

Freedom is the key to being happy in life and it is not possible to be truly happy in life if you are limited and if there are a lot of things you are unable to do for arbitrary reasons.

The Power of Gratitude

There is more to happiness that can be gained from minimalism. Minimalism comes down to the realization that you have all that you need in order to be happy no matter what your current circumstances are. You don't need to constantly be chasing that next thing and then slowly going back to the default level of happiness once you acquire it. When you are constantly chasing the next thing, you will realize that you never really stop to smell the roses and to appreciate what you have.

What you have to train yourself to do is to develop an appreciation of how lucky you are already by living in such a prosperous time. You need to develop and practice gratitude. The simple way to achieve this is to take time and to think of everything you own and the reasons you should feel grateful because of that. It doesn't have to take more than a couple of minutes. It is good to have it written down in some kind of notepad so that you can remind yourself of that.

You want to try to add things to your gratitude list and you will get better at this over time since there are a lot of cool things to be grateful for. Your health is wealth and you should be grateful for that. You can be grateful if you have people who care about you. You can also be grateful for the fact that you have a place where you can spend your night.

In order to make being grateful easier, you want to regularly do things you enjoy by following the list of enjoyable activities which you compiled earlier. You have to be really enjoying the things on the list and it can be whatever you want, whether it's admiring the night sky or helping your kids build a sand castle.

You need some creativity when making this list so that you utilize the things you already have in order to have a good time. You only have to look around you a bit to get a lot of ideas on how to have a good time.

No matter what you do, you need to reflect on how happy you are to be in a situation that you are in. You want to get to the point when you are living presently and mindfully in the moment and not worrying about what's next or about what was and this is a pretty important spiritual concept. You don't want to allow your mind to go astray since that will inevitably lead you to your worries which will make it harder to enjoy what you are currently doing. When you are in a museum or an art gallery or someplace similar, you want to be able to truly appreciate what is in front of you.

Another challenge is to slow down during your breakfast so that you can actually take in and realize how much enjoyment you are actually getting out of it. You will also be enjoying your meal a whole lot more if you anticipate it beforehand. Regardless of what your meal will be, it will be so much better if you create some anticipation. It is all about knowing how to really appreciate good things in life and in this way you are letting more value into your life and this can be done regardless of how much money you have and this can be a difference between a non-wealthy person who is a happy and miserable wealthy person.

Conclusion of Minimalism Home

I hope that this book has provided you with an understanding of minimalism and the ways in which you can use it to make your life better. It may seem like all this book is about is removing some clutter here and there so that you can start to properly enjoy what is important to you. You have to know what you want out of life in order to formulate a plan that will get you there. Minimalism, however, is also about designing a home that serves you and which helps you in reaching your goals by making things easy for you via elimination of obstacles and clutter such as debt.

I hope that, by now, you have developed an inspiration for turning your home into something entirely new by just getting rid of the unnecessary stuff and the financial burden of having to keep it all together. I know that you have some unique ideas on how would you design your home so that it looks luxurious while also adding your own flavor to it.

But in order to do this, you first have to accept it in your mind that you don't need a lot in order to be happy regardless of what the media are telling you. The actual truth is that a lot of stuff which you have might actually be making you less happy and causing you stress and stopping you from doing what you truly want since your current expenses are so high.

A lot of things which you thought you wanted, you probably may not even have wanted since the idea of you wanting a certain item was placed in your head by advertising. You want to take control back and you can do so by creating a deliberate plan for achieving your vision. This way you will only be spending on what is getting you closer to the goal and the lifestyle which you want to have.

You need to be patient and to keep hope alive because one day you will break out of the loop of always wanting the next thing and your mindset will be transformed so that you could be happy. The whole process of going minimal is a journey and you can start it right now and without any cost by getting rid of those things you know don't serve you anymore.

Declutter and Organize

Live Intentionally by Decluttering Your Home and Life, Doing More With Less and Focusing on What is Essential in Your Life

By Matt Mckinney

Introduction to Declutter and Organize

Most people buy things which they don't need to impress people they don't like at all. That's the life of most people. It may sound harsh, but it's true. People think that having more makes the life somehow better.

Quality of life is measured by what is owned. Some people also base their self worth on their possessions. You should remember that price doesn't equate value. Just because something costs more, it doesn't mean that it has more value and it will make someone's life more worthwhile.

A lot of people prioritize what is expected of them instead of what they actually want themselves. Certain values that people live by weren't even chosen by them, they were implanted by someone else.

Too many children simply live their lives based on what their parents want without any challenge or rebuttal. Maybe they don't even see that there is something to be challenged in the first place. As long as parents do and think something in a certain way, then that's all there is to it.

There isn't any inquiry into whether the whole life plan makes sense or not and whether there is a better way entirely. It is not even considered if a certain way of life makes sense in the current times. It is just assumed that a certain path is the best one since all the loved and respected people are walking it.

People in first world countries are not necessarily happy due to way too much stress and credit card debt. It seems that it's harder and harder to become content. Cluttered lives may limit the amount of joy which can be achieved in life and a lot of people aren't even aware of this.

Chapter 1: The Pitfalls of Clutter

Stress limits someone's effectiveness and it hurts relationships. The job also isn't done as well as it could be and challenges are a bigger deal than they should be. Life is not supposed to be easy and surprises are inevitable. It is all about preparation and how these surprises are handled.

However, there is a lot of entitlement and expectation that life should be smooth and easy. That is why it can be so easy to be stressed and so hard to be happy for some. The focus is always on what can be acquired in the future. Focus is placed on everything except the present, such as past failures. It is a never ending search for something to blame for why things are the way they are.

This is an example of mental clutter and a lot of people accept it as a part of life and as a statement of their self worth and their identity. In reality, mental clutter isn't something that is supposed to be a part of life and it doesn't appear by itself or by mere bad luck.

The precursor to the mental clutter is the physical clutter and this is how a never ending mental loop is established. The more mental clutter there is, the more physical clutter tends to be created. A mere sight of this causes stress and more mental clutter. This process has no end by itself.

A lot of us have no clue about this whole loop. If there is some form of unhappiness in your life, there is possibility that the source of that unhappiness could be traced back to mental clutter. This loop can prevent people for achieving happiness and other life goals.

Too many people will make excuses as they are not even aware of this loop. A resistance is also put up against any attempt to simplify things and to state how a lot of things are a little more than an unnecessary burden. The Resistance exists as a defense of the identity which is dependent on the possession of a lot of stuff.

Most people will respond to any decluttering attempt similarly. People have to want to change in order to change. Accepting that change is necessary and really internalizing that are two different things. Internalizing this fact creates urgency and that is how things really get done without justifications.

A lot of people stay stuck at simply knowing that change is necessary in order to achieve happiness and their potential in life. They also know what they should stop doing because its's wrong. It is important for this understanding to sink to the heart in order to make real progress. It is necessary to achieve true belief.

What is involved?

You are not the only one affected by clutter since you can't completely keep all the emotions to yourself which means that other people will be affected. Relationships are inevitably affected by this whole interaction between possessions and internal states. If someone is filled with harmful emotions, ideas and attitudes as a result of all the clutter, it is way too easy for something to leak out and cause things that ruin relationships such as misunderstandings and misconceptions.

Relationships won't be automatically doomed, but they may start going downhill by becoming more passive-aggressive which could cause each side to sabotage the other just for the sake of sticking it to the other side.

Relationships should be about building each other up in every way, and not about a destructive loop. Stress causes stress to spread to more people and in this way, the cycle never ends and it's like a downward spiral. This also doesn't end because people also feel that they will be in a disadvantage if they stop doing what they have always done.

Thankfully, there is a simple way to break out of this. All it takes is to be proactive and to decide to deal with clutter in order to create your ideal life. Anyone can do this regardless of their age. It is never too late or too early to start decluttering your life.

Chapter 2: You Can Take Action Against The Clutter

There is some discouragement upon the realization that a lot of issues are caused by clutter. No matter what the nature of clutter is, clutter has a lot of influence even among the most resilient people. A lot of people probably realize that they are dealing with too many things. Those things may be from the past or from the future.

There is a lot of fear and worry when it comes to decluttering. People know that too many things are bad and they don't need someone else to remind them of that. The weird thing is that people get attached to clutter to the point where they can't imagine a simpler life.

A lot of people underestimate the power of decluttering and they consider it as nothing more than an impractical speculation. The truth is that the results can be achieved by decluttering and that the positive impact can be clearly seen and accomplished by anyone.

Why is Doing This Necessary?

Even if people realize that they should declutter, they may ask themselves if it is even worth the effort although they understand that the clutter may be behind their struggle and suffering.

To the people who have already decluttred, the benefits are obvious. Decluttering enables someone to be more effective, as simple as that may sound. It's hard to be effective under constant worry and fear. Relationships also suffer because of that.

The unhappiness because of clutter manifests itself sooner or later and completely dilutes the focus. It is easier to be content by decluttering and this makes it easier to focus on what matters and this is how freedom is achieved. There is no freedom in worrying all the time about what happened or about what might happen.

You have a lot of potential and you can create the reality which you want, for better or worse. You can either box yourself in or you can create a life of freedom and possibilities for yourself.

There are steps which you can take in order to recognize all the clutter you may be dealing with. Don't skip the steps and take as much time as you need. Only move on to the next step when you have mastered the previous. Only move on to the next step when the current one becomes easy.

The steps are the following and an entire chapter is dedicated to each step. Step 1 is understanding what's going on. Step 2 is to start with what is in front of you. Step 3 is to declutter emotionally. Step 4 is to declutter psychologically. Step 5 is decluttering careerwise. Step 6 is learning how to get more out of less. Step 7 is learning how to be content.

Some flexibility can be applied to these steps since all people are different. Know what your situation is and customize accordingly. The formula which is outlined is not a perfect one and it is necessary to have self-awareness in order to make it work according to your specific circumstances.

The formula in this book is not something that will fit all sizes and you are unlikely to find anything of that sort. What is presented is more akin to the framework which requires active involvement in order to achieve personal success with decluttering.

Chapter 3: Understand What's Going On

To declutter, you have to understand what your life situation is and build a strategy around that. The strategy is focused on reducing clutter since getting rid of clutter entirely isn't possible. You will just end up disappointed if you expect to get rid of clutter entirely. Clutter reduction is the goal.

You may not have the proper perspective due to the amount of clutter around you right now and this may make it harder for you to make sense of your place in this world and your capabilities to act within it. You need a strategy for decluttering in order to stop spending money on things you don't need to impress people you don't like.

If you don't know where to start, then check your life against 5 signs of a cluttered life to see whether you are dealing with clutter. Clutter is easy to see at first, but later people get used to it and blends with the background as it becomes the default.

Decluttering should be gradual so that your perspective could adjust accordingly. You should give your perspective enough time to adjust since your attitude and relationships depend on it.

Sign of a Cluttered Life: Angst

Do you have a feeling that you are missing something no matter what you may be doing and who you may be doing it with? It feels like a piece is always missing. Something just isn't right and it is starting to mess with your head.

This feeling comes and goes. At times it is very noticeable and at times it is very subtle and you can feel it somewhere in the background. This feeling annoys you and you can't exactly put your finger on it, but you know it's there and you get used to it over time.

Sign of a Cluttered Life: Anxiety

Do you worry and think of bad scenarios too much? You worry about how people may react and how some things in the future may turn out. The reality is that things usually tend to go a lot better than the disaster you come up within your mind and you should get a sense of relief at the end. People with anxiety never feel this sense of relief and they immediately start thinking about the next disaster. It's hard to be happy or content this way.

This never ends and there is always some form of anticipation about something bad that could happen in the future. When the situation clears up, anxious people start to worry about something else. Anxiety can make people physically sick sometimes. It is necessary to have some calming ritual to get things under control.

Sign of a Cluttered Life: It's Never Enough

Have you ever thought about what makes you happy? Have you also thought about how you would be happier upon getting more of that stuff that gets you happy? A lot of people think that their life will be complete if they just got the next thing such as a new car or a bigger house or something similar.

When those things are acquired, the happiness doesn't last and inevitably people start wanting more stuff again. There is some science to this and money can make people happy, no matter what you may have been hearing. You can get a rush out of buying things, but that feeling is fleeting and after that, you will want more stuff.

This is similar to a rush from sugar or cocaine. You feel great in the beginning, but it won't last and you will try to get it again and it will never be as good as the first time. The first time you buy a car, for example, is special and it is unlikely to feel as good afterward. This all works acording to the law of diminishing returns.

It's easy to get into a routine of buying new things just to get the rush when the old things stop functioning perfectly. The first time is always like magic, though and there is a true sense of discovery and a lot of details tend to be remembered vividly for a long time.

When you buy something new, you get a rush and you are happy. It feels great, without a doubt, but it's temporary and the crash is inevitable. After the crash, the rush wants to be reexperienced and the only way is to buy more. The hole never seems to be filled and it all feels like a hamster wheel.

Sign of a Cluttered Life: You are Never Satisfied

Did you ever take the time to sit down and think about how much you have done and how much you have and concluded, based on that, that you have enough. Chances are high that the answer to that is negative. It's way easier to look over the shoulder.

What the neighbors are doing and why you aren't doing the same thing always seems to be on the mind. The grass always seems to be greener and everyone seems to be happier of Facebook.

It seems that your accomplishments, however great they may be, are never enough. There's always the feeling of more value and worth being out there. The search for bigger and shinier things never ends.

Sign of a Cluttered Life: You are Scared You Will Lose Everything

It is interesting how many people don't feel they have enough in combination with the fear of losing it all. Isn't it ironic?

These are all the signs of a cluttered life. It's hard to live a life with purpose and meaning with all the mental and physical clutter. Days just blend together without much purpose and it gets hard telling days apart and remembering much.

When life is like this from day to day, then buying stuff starts to be the only thing someone looks forward to, but after the rush had worn off, more stuff is wanted. It feels like you are running in circles with no end in sight.

Start by Figuring out What Matters to You

Now is time to figure out what is important to you. You will probably find out that stuff and possessions aren't the most important things to you. You should ask yourself what is truly important and what you would go to the end of the world for. You are the only one who can determine what is important to you based on your values and experiences.

This is a big question and some assistance may be necessary in order to get the to the answers. In order to get to those answers, you can utilize a value audit which will simplify things for you.

Value Audit

Auditing your values is simple and you don't need anything more than a piece of paper and a pen. Write down what you would do if money wasn't an issue and if you didn't care what others would think in the slightest.

Don't filter anything out and write the first thing that comes to mind. This is all about you and there are no right and wrong answers. Don't think about what others may think and try to compile a list of things that drive you. Put everything on the list without editing no matter how embarrassing or negative something may be.

What you have written down are your values and they subconsciously guide your thoughts and actions throughout the day. These values give you energy and they get you out of bed each day and give you meaning. Finding out those values is important and that is the purpose of an audit.

Do a Detox

Now that you know what is important, ask yourself why it may be important to you. It may give your life a sense of meaning or purpose. Maybe it just unleashes your imagination. It could also make you more adventurous.

You also have to ask yourself why do you like the things you like. Is it possible that your parents told you what is desirable, and how things should be done and how life is meant to be perceived? Are your perspective and your values influenced by other people?

Your values should be your choice. A lot of things you think you need may just be a result of someone else's expectations. It can be way too easy to keep doing things because that's the way they were done all along.

In order to get started, you should make a list of values that are truly yours. Next, make sure to make a list of values which you adopted externally. You detox by focusing on your own values and getting away from those which aren't yours. The decluttering starts when you let go of the external and focus on your values.

Chapter 4: How to Start

Decluterring starts with what you can see and touch. Get rid of stuff that causes any form of clutter in your life. This isn't as easy as it sounds since possessions have a way of taking hold of people. You need a plan since you may start missing things once they are gone.

You need any kind of plan since you are very likely to fail if you fail to plan. Decluttering is no exception to this. Know why you are trying to achieve what you are trying to achieve. You may come to the conclusion that your possessions are holding you back and that they are sapping your energy. It is not easy realizing that things you worked so hard for may be the main culprit.

You will realize the difficulty of decluttering when you ask yourself do you really want to get rid of a certain item even if you know that it is holding you down. It is easy to stay trapped since you may be attached to certain things emotionally.

The plan will help you realize what you are trying to accomplish and why you are doing things. Your commitment will be stronger if you write it down. When something unexpected happens, as it always does, it is way too easy to forget about priorities and that is why it is so crucial to think ahead and to write things down. Make sure to read over your writing each and every morning.

It will be inevitably hard to let some things go, but you will be good as long as you stick to your plan. Consistency is the most important thing when it comes to plans and the lack of it can be the end of even the best of plans. The sad fact is that most people fail at decluttering with carrying out their decluttering plan and it is not for the lack of resources and intelligence.

The cause of this failure is not sticking with the plan. Sticking with the plan is all it takes and there is no need to complicate it. If you have a plan, then you have clarity about what you should do each day to reach your goals. It is necessary not to deviate from the plan regardless of what may be happening.

There is bound to be a lot of resistance since most people define themselves according to their possessions. That is just how it is. When you are long enough around certain external things, those things start to define you and they can also be a limit when it comes to your capabilities. Having a plan which you can see each day is the first step

Change You Personal Patterns

It is necessary to clear up a couple of misconceptions. This book isn't about getting rid of everything and living like a monk away from the civilization. It is about changing your philosophy about stuff. Stuff has the hold of you when you start allowing it to define you as an individual.

This happens all the time and most people tend to define themselves based on consumption. Ironically, the consumption never seems to truly fulfill them. The hunger within them never ends.

You may have only been able to afford 2 simple meals a day at one point of your life. You may have been quite content with it at the time even if there were so many better things out there. That just shows that you don't necessarily need a lot of stuff to be happy as long as you have people around you who care about you and with whom you can spend quality time with. None of this requires a lot of money.

If you are not careful, your life may end up being more and more expensive and this is, in part, due to changing expectations. It's easy to think that having a luxurious apartment is the only way to get ahead and be worthy.

Every graduation and every promotion has a way of driving up the cost and it never ends. The truth is as simple as that. When you think about it, is having a Ferrari and a huge house worth all the sacrifice? That is what you have to answer yourself, but the focus should always be on what you really need. Everyone will require a personalized solution.

You can only create a plan once you start thinking about what you really need. Once you have that foundation, that is when you start creating your relationships and possessions anew.

When you have a plan, you have to adhere to the plan no matter what may be happening and no matter how you may be feeling. Just think about how better your life would be if you changed your relationship with your possessions. That will make it easier for you to stay committed.

Whenever you buy something again, you will have a better sense of why you are buying a certain item. Now it is time to declutter and to let go of the things weighing you down.

Just Do It!

At this point, you have a commitment and a plan. You know what you have to do and why. Use to 8020 principle as there is a good chance that 20% of the stuff is responsible for 80% of your personal results. If you look at all your stuff, there is a good chance of that being the case.

Most of the stuff doesn't really do much more than being nice to look at. The 20% that contributes to your results the most is what you also use most often. These things are also likely to fullfill you and make you content o a great extent.

When it comes to the remaining 80%, you have to get rid of it and this will be easier if you list those things based on how emotionally attached to them you are. The stuff which you care the least about is the stuff you want to get rid of first. It gets trickier as you move up the list. You have to stick to the plan and think about how those things are weighing you down. This whole process is easier if you remain focused on the 20% of stuff as a source of positivity.

Don't Forget What is Important

This whole process is not easy and improvements wont be noticed immediately upon its completion. Thats just not how it is. The whole process is for nothing unless you stick to the plan since that is the only way to prevent the clutter from returning to your life after the declutter.

It is not just about getting rid of things, it is about changing the mindset and your philosophy about things and life. This is the hard and uncomfortable part. Deviate from the plan may be very tempting when you come across some new fancy gadget. This is when commitment is tested.

Decluttering isnt just about getting rid of stuff, it is also about remaining clear of previous habits and acquisition patterns.

Don't Skip Anything

It's simple to remove things that are undoubtedly status symbols. It's simple to do away with things that are clearly gadgets, trinkets, and things which really don't include very much value besides maybe some kind of mental reward. Take a look at things which give you pleasure. There's a ton to deal with there.

You need to recognize that if an object gives you pleasure, you are simply utilizing that thing as some kind of mental mirror. Genuine pleasure, confidence and a feeling of worth or significance can only come from within. You're utilizing that thing as a prop.

Your task is to get rid of the object and go directly to the root cause. It is you providing yourself that meaning. Remove the middle man. Pay attention to what's within. Shortly after you have done away with the 80% of tangible clutter, you need to begin considering all your other possessions. This could be non-material. I'm referring to mindsets, mental patterns, psychological clutter, beliefs, assumptions, fallacies.

Believe it or not, these are tougher to deal with. As I pointed out, a great deal of the physical things which we purchase are effectively just mirrors. Their true worth is based upon what's happening in our heads. They help remind us of the ideas which we hold in our heads.

Remove those ideas, and you would not require things that embodies that. As unpleasant as cleaning up a bunch of these physical belongings can be, this doesn't match up to the type of heavy lifting that you will need to do within your head.

Chapter 5: Getting Rid of Mental Clutter

As I pointed out in the intro to this book, your physical clutter sets off the emotional clutter. Emotional clutter, consequently, sets off other manner of inner clutter, which drives you to participate in hoarding habits, or whatever else can result in physical clutter.

This tangible clutter then speaks to your inner clutter, and the entire procedure replays itself again. You're transmitting all the negative signals to yourself, and you wind up considering and carrying out things which steer you additionally down this hole.

You need to take the following step and take care of this inner clutter. Or else, despite the amount of stuff you eliminated of your life, you are going to ultimately return to where you began. By and large, the tangible clutter which we create or stockpile in our lives is just a stand-in for our emotional concerns.

We purchase things not due to the fact we require it but due to the fact we read all kinds of meanings into it. In case you are searching for a car, you could do equally as well purchasing a Kia. It keeps you nice and cozy, and dry whenever it's raining outdoors. Simply put, it deals with the basics, however folks don't purchase Kia's. Rather, they crave and want Lamborghini's, Ferrari's, BMWs, Mercedes Benzes, Maserati's.

In short, you're not actually purchasing stuff due to the necessities that purchase tackles. Rather, you're purchasing stuff thanks to the emotional signs or mental reality you're reading into. There is a call-and-response pattern here. You purchase things due to the fact that you're feeling unfulfilled within.

The more things you possess, the more you require since you keep nourishing that emotional gap that is constantly craving. You need to take care of that emotional gap after you've dealt with the physical part of clutter. You do this by changing your mentally upsetting habits. This is the initial step.

If you invest a great deal of time with social media, that is not a good use of your energy. When folks publish their updates, they're displaying to you images of their "perfect life." No one will upload video footage of them getting fired from their job or any other event that is just as bad. No person does that, at least no one in their right frame of mind.

Rather, what you get are pictures of the parts of their life which are heading the right way. You get a wonderful photo of a family heading out for dinner. Everyone outfitted really nice. You get delightful, underhanded pictures of the new BMW in the garage.

They are going to think of imaginative ways to let you learn about their new achievement. Perhaps someone would post "Have a look at the new bicycle I got," and they have a truly lovely, decent-looking bike, and directly behind it is a Bentley. You know how this works.

Sadly, if you saturate yourself in that sort of stimuli, you are captured in a social signal "soup". You're basically comparing the actuality of your life with the misleading truth proposed by other folks. It's a losing game. They're in excellent shape considering that they're presenting you the aspect of their life that is proceeding in the right direction. They don't display to you HIV or cancer or addictions. They demonstrate to you the ideal part of their lives. As a matter of fact, a bunch of folks who do this, do it to comfort themselves. They're just saying to themselves, "Somehow some way at the very least one thing is going well in my existence."

The issue is you're absorbing this all up and the message that you're receiving is: "My life stinks compared to that person." The comical feature of comparison, at least in a social media framework, is that irrespective of what you possess and no matter how good you have it going, it is never going to ever amount to what you are seeing. Whenever you compare and contrast, you find yourself on the losing side since you don't concentrate on whatever it is you have. Rather, your focus heads to what's lacking, and it all leads to the identical destination. You don't have enough.

That's the story you keep instilling in your brain when you participate in emotionally straining habits such as social media. Even if you were to get rid of your Twitter or Facebook accounts, you're nevertheless going to encounter this if you associate with folks who boast about stuff that's working out in their lives.

A ton of individuals who do this don't actually do this to put you down. Actually, a great deal of them feel truly unconfident and without control. Therefore, what do they do? They accentuate the aspects that are going their way. And here you are absorbing it all in, and you take anything they say literally and because of that you wind up missing out. You find yourself coming up short. That's the way comparisons function.

This is a quite harmful environment, and you don't need to be on social media to experience this. You ought to tone down or get rid of your social media accounts, and you ought to stop spending time around toxic individuals.

The Bottom Line

Removing emotional clutter truly comes down to monitoring what you feed your emotions. You need to recognize that whatever you pick up has an impact on your mental state. Sadly, a ton of folks are really negligent concerning what they feed their brain. They believe they're merely checking out what's going on and catching up.

The issue is if you possess the inappropriate perspective, you wind up placing yourself in a more stressful spot. It doesn't truly matter what you have going your way. Assuming that you possess the inappropriate attitude, you are going to always find yourself at the losing end of that contrast.

Even the most productive and wealthiest people on the planet can make themselves feel depressed by means of comparison. Stay clear of that comparison frame of mind. It's fine to socialize with a bunch of folks, but if your attitude leads you to do this, at that point you deteriorate yourself. Monitor what you feed your mind with.

It all comes down to your attitude. When folks are saying anything to you, you could definitely interpret it a neutral way. You could also read it in a constructive manner. You could place a twist on it that elevates you, motivates you or invigorates you. This is easier said than done. Actually, folks interpret things in the worst manner conceivable and they feel worse when it comes to themselves.

Bear in mind who you involve yourself with, what you concentrate on and, essentially, how you interpret things. The trick to this truly all comes down to taking care of your emotional habits. A great deal of our mental habits are passed down from our parents. We are, besides, primarily products of our enviroment.

Nevertheless, simply due to the fact that your past is a particular way doesn't essentially indicate that you need to die with that same past. The big undertaking of life is to conquer previous programming. you were born in poverty and coping doesn't automatically indicate you have to die like that. It all comes down to observing what you give to your emotions.

Inevitably, you ought to arrive at the point where no matter how antagonistic people are around you, your positive psychological patterns allow you to counteract that feedback. Rather than beating yourself up, you could perhaps even make use of this feedback to drive yourself ahead. To kick off the process, you need to initially zero in on five harmful emotional habits to reduce and after that get rid of these from your life.

Harmful Emotional Habit # 1: Regularly comparing yourself to other people

You need to recognize that folks commonly compare themselves to other people. We're sort of genetically inclined to do this. But why?

Well, imagine thousands of years ago and you and a friend are strolling down a path and one of you notices a bear. You see that your friend begins warming up as if he's exercising for a race.

You ask him, "Are you insane? You will never outrun that bear. You understand how quick bears are." Your buddy would after that explain to you, "I don't have to be quicker than the bear. I just have to be quicker than you."

This classic joke emphasizes the reality that folks are comparative naturally. Whenever people stop contrasting themselves to others, it's highly probable that they won't invest sufficient energy, and their genes are going to vanish. Even so, we arrived at an age in which a lot of our fundamental requirements are handled by technology and present-day markets. Now is the moment to do away with this default propensity to continuously compare yourself to other people.

You ought to proactively interrupt this type of thought patterns. One of the absolute most effective approaches to mess up comparative thinking is to become more outward-directed. For example, if you end up seeing an old friend you haven't seen in a while, make an effort to be more enthusiastic and say, "You haven't aged one day", without making any comparison between you two.

Transform your evaluation and your psychological focus on the other individual. This is among the ideal things you could possibly do since not only does this make the other individual feel far better and this could go a very long way in sealing your relationship. It additionally refocuses your thoughts from your usual inclination to compare.

Direct more of your interest to other people. Be a lot more outward-directed. Simply put, be more caring. When you have the ability to accomplish this, you're evaluating yourself less.

Harmful Emotional Habit # 2: Drawing Mental Prizes from Material Belongings

Whenever you take a look at the things which you own, stop examining them in emotional terms. When you take a look at your most-prized belongings, appreciate them depending on their own inherent properties.

Rather than looking into the logo of the vehicle which sits in your garage and ways in which that logo evokes all kinds of "elite" or "status" images, value your things for what they perform and the issues they deal with.

Take a look at the smooth lines, also check out the remarkable engineering and you're just admiring how incredible the makers are. You get out of your cycle of worry and your necessity to continuously reinforce self-esteem.

Rather, you get pulled into a remarkable technological trip consisting of the sort of engineering required to get into the item. Do you see how this works? The identical goes for any other type of luxury product.

Whenever you do this, you concentrate not just on the product but also the individuals responsible for it. You're making wonderful progress the moment you begin imagining along these lines due to the fact that you're no longer thinking of yourself.

Typically, when folks take a look at status symbols, they consider the item actually like a mirror. They take a look at the bag which has an item logo on it and consider how rich they are, how other individuals would admire them etc.

None of this mental dialogue actually has something to do with the bag in itself. It's just about you, and the more you concentrate on yourself, the more you're caught on that ego void, and it worsens as time goes on.

Begin considering material things on the basis of their terms, not based upon the mental rewards you receive due to the fact that you have them. This is the way you make progress in your quest to owning things rather than having things own you.

Harmful Emotional Habit # 3: Immediately Thinking that a Hefty Price Tag Indicates Higher Value

A bunch of folks mistake price with value. Prices are established by means of demand and supply. Whenever there is a constrained supply and there a considerable amount of demand, the price increases. In a similar way, even when there's a substantial supply, if the demand is substantial enough or consistent enough, the price increases.

This likewise works in reverse. A bunch of folks have this notion that demand is basically a product of need. Whenever the price of pasta or wheat, for instance, increases and folks presume that it's as a result of need. The reality is that demand could likewise entail perceived demand. Simply put, the assumption of value by folks demanding a specific product due to the fact that in economics there is something known as substitution.

You could be assuming that the demand for wheat is fixed, however, you need to also bear in mind that folks are able to substitute or switch rice, potatoes or other types of wheat for starch. I introduce this to your awareness due to the fact that a large aspect of demand consists of group perception. The more you could persuade folks that a particular item has worth, no matter how plentiful that item is, its price is going to increase.

A typical instance of this is the diamond industry. Did you know that diamonds are in fact quite plentiful? That's correct. This crystallized sort of carbon is really not that uncommon. However, because of the DeBeers cartel working out of South Africa in addition to long-running, extensive advertising campaigns, diamonds have ended up being very pricey.

It should not be as costly as it is. This is because of fabricated demand. Just because a thing has a higher price doesn't always imply it has worth as far as you are concerned. Its greater cost might be because of some kind of group deception like diamond price.

When you view Ralph Lauren print advertisements, they make an effort to get you to invest into a way of life. A great deal of these photos just present certainly attractive people in spectacular locations and perhaps some of those individuals would be sporting the actual product that's being promoted.

Rather, you see this truly captivating model looking to the side like he or she has a concern. This is deliberate. The true item here is the way of life that you're expected to invest into since it's so incredible, it's so separate from your way of life. Your life is mundane. These models' lifestyles, however, are exotic.

They are appealing to what's lacking in your way of life. Your life consists of nine-to-five regimens. You turn up to work, you work your eight hours and then you head home. Rinse and repeat. Absolutely, every now and then, you embark on a vacation and have a go at anything fresh, but that's your life.

That's how they advertise to folks. Abercrombie and Fitch turn this into a scientific discipline. They show you this different life which you might have, and you experience it the second you purchase their goods. This item is the entrance to this way of life or adventure.

You just have to take a look at the billions of dollars being invested annually or lifestyle marketing to get your truth. The worst component to this advertising is that it delivers the point that your life is not sufficiently good. There is something superior out there, but you have to purchase our item to arrive.

If we take people's word that they really purchase things since it fits well, the truth is that there are heaps of other apparel lines out there which fit properly. What makes this company any different? It truly all comes down to marketing.

Nonetheless, if you take a look at the fabric, the design and whatever else, it's truly tough to warrant shelling out $200 on a pair of jeans when you could purchase it for $30 from a different brand or a no-name brand. The difference is in the sold lifestyle.

I bring this stuff up since this is what pumps up perceived value. It's smart. It reveals the genius behind these large brands but, eventually, there's very little distinction between a $300 pair of jeans and a $30 pair. They need to fool folks into believing that higher price implies high value.

Taking into consideration that there is a multibillion-dollar high-end goods industry stretching throughout various industry verticals tells you everything you have to understand about how prevalent this programming is. The smartphone you have in your pocket is proof positive of this. If you're just trying to find features, you most likely would be better off with an android mobile phone that costs all of $50.

There's truly no convincing reason you ought to shell out more than $500 on a smartphone that has a lovely little logo. Regretfully, this results in emotionally harmful habits. You must never beat yourself up over the reality that you can not load your life with high-price-tag products as price isn't always an indication of value.

The only worth any product can deliver is the worth you give to it. This procedure again shows how the marketplace functions since pricing systems don't work based upon the amount of work someone invests in a product.

Karl Marx is completely incorrect. Based upon his book, Das Kapital, the true price of any item is the amount of work that is invested there. Even if you invested two thousand hours to developing a product, however, when you place it on the marketplace, nobody wishes to purchase it. How much money is that product actually worth? A great deal of nothing.

Pricing is established by demand. The price of something is anything that you read into it. It stems from you. You must bust the fabricated link around price and value which is established by the other individuals. You beat yourself up to purchase that item since you wish to be highly valued.

You have your own inherent value. No matter what you wear. Think about your own self like a hundred-dollar bill. If I had a hundred-dollar bill before you and spit on it, trample on it with my boot, fold it, toss it around, how much do you believe that hundred-dollar bill is worth?

It's still a hundred dollars. Certain folks are going to grab it since they recognize value when they experience it. The identical goes for you. You might be dressed in rags. You might seem all disorganized. Nevertheless, you still possess value. Always keep this in your mind. Now, the key to all of this is the only individual that uncovers your value is yourself. If you act like a high-value individual, folks are going to value you. In the end, this really all comes down to your choice and your judgments.

Harmful Emotional Habit # 4: Focusing on "Drawing Out" the Benefits People Have Rather Than Viewing Them as Whole People

Do you socialize with folks who are energy vampires? These individuals socialize with you only to absorb your positive vibrations. They don't add a thing. All they speak about are their issues. They spend time around you because they wish to feel great. You speak of things that are heading in the right direction, and they cruise on this positivity. These individuals are drawing out good energy from you.

They view you merely as a host. They are energy barnacles. You perhaps do this too at a certain degree or another or in one style. It's really uncommon that you encounter someone who only likes to socialize with you due to who you are. They possess a great deal of abundance in their life, and it streams to the outside.

Sadly, the majority of folks are not like that. Rather, we socialize with people to obtain things. Now, it would blow to associate with folks who attempt to squeeze money from you. Nevertheless, this takes one other shape. These are individuals who are psychological vampires. All they talk about are their issues. They discuss matters that are not going well.

In addition, other individuals like to stir your own insecurities due to the fact that they're unconfident. They hope that by talking about their frustrations you will talk about theirs. These folks only wish to believe that there are other individuals as unhappy as them all over the world.

Perhaps at first, it feels awesome. But, the more you activate each other's pessimism, the further you create harmful psychological energy between you. Rather than your friendship allowing both of you to leave this emotional hole, you really wind up giving one another shovels.

You need to dispose of this particularly harmful emotional habit. Why? The more you draw out from someone else, the less probably you will fix your own troubles. All you're accomplishing is just assuring yourself with what is primarily bad in your life without truly doing this to fix it at long last.

You're certainly not challenging yourself. Rather, you're enclosed deeper inside your comfort zone, and you're just reiterating this pessimism or you're drawing out some kind of emotional peace of mind from your buddy.

Hazardous Emotional Habit # 5: Freeloading Emotionally Off People

Have you ever socialized with folks who think just like you? You might be considering that this is a beneficial thing. Sadly, that sense of belonging has limitations. There is something as a comfy prison. Whenever you're hanging out with folks who just strengthen your worst assumptions, you're not really helping yourself.

You wind up speaking and preaching to the choir. No one advances. No person challenges their viewpoints. No one enhances their possibilities of bursting out of this psychological imprisonment. You need to recognize that psychological prisons end up being more limiting when folks who reside in the network with one another.

There is some kind of emotional reward. Nonetheless, you're paying a strong price for it. You're strengthening one another's preferences. If you do not trust me, focus on a friend who you are emotionally freeloading off or who's doing so to you. Keep track of the topics you speak of. I'm ready to wager a great deal of money that you discuss the identical things over and over again.

This is harmful. You're not challenging one another to leave the emotional mess. Rather, you're again allowing one another dig a much deeper hole. Partly, this is actually comparable to the five harmful emotional habits I explained above. A great deal of the folks who have those damaging emotional patterns are the identical as individuals who I'm going to illustrate.

The results are identical. They lead you to an unpleasant place. They strengthen all your nastiest emotional habits. Identify the following five kinds of harmful people in your life and begin distancing yourself from these guys. This does not always indicate that you need to cut them off completely. You just need to grant yourself ample distance.

You still chat with them every now and then, but they're not so near and so dear that they wind up pulling you down. At the minimum, you're not so attached to them that you are caught in this descending emotional spiral.

Harmful Personality Type # 1: The Black Hole

This individual has deep emotional requirements. They're really needy individuals. You can't tell by their look. Some appear quite successful. Nevertheless, when they open up their mouths to someone they believe that they can count on, it's all about them, them and them.

It's as though any sort of support, any type of convenience or any type of emotional help simply won't measure up. Even though you provide and provide, it's nonetheless insufficient since that's how they are. They are black holes. Do yourself a big one. Steer clear from black holes. I'm not claiming that you ought to cut them out, but don't get so close. Why? Picture a spacecraft or a planet getting next to a black hole. What do you think happens?

Harmful Personality Type # 2: The Judge

Do you have a buddy or an associate who's regularly placing everyone and everything into neat, orderly, small boxes. This may not appear all that damaging initially. Nevertheless, this habit of theirs could be quite harmful since existence is not black and white.

It's easy to believe that when someone develops a negative opinion that it's unreasonable contrasted to when someone has a fantastic impression of you and states, "Oh, you're a champion." Well, suppose I informed you that they are equally harmful? Why? People are people. We change constantly. There are numerous edges to us and to minimize somebody into a one-word summary really empties them of their humanity.

Regrettably, none of the subtlety matters to the judge. He or she obtains a significant amount of pleasure in rendering his or her world as black and white as feasible. Either someone is a loser or someone is a winner. There's no midpoint. You don't essentially need to stop being pals with these people, but attain some kind of space because, eventually, you begin embracing that black-and-white frame of mind, and this is very destructive due to the fact that the world is not black and white. It's actually so vivid, so dynamic and so stunning.

Harmful Personality Type # 3: The Stylish Hoarder

The style hoarder is an individual who checks out various people's lives and looks for patterns or styles which they can gather. When you talk with this person, they're not truly curious about the genuine you. They couldn't care less concerning your expectations, goals, fears, ambitions, insecurities.

Rather, they evaluate what you are doing. They're consumed with all kinds of trends. These could be technical trends, style trends. Nonetheless, it's things which various other people are doing.

They then utilize this as some kind of framework when they're judging you, and they claim, "Ah, this person, does he think in this manner? Does he cooperate in that trend? Does he have this style understanding that is sort of trendy?"

You pretty much prove their verdicts regarding trends since they're drawing out a large awareness of their self-worth and pride from that. They really feel great about having the ability to identify these trends. They feel good about belonging to the appropriate group or individuals who think the appropriate ideas.

However, the inspiration is very superficial. It's truly all about making themselves feel great, feel significant and feel deserving. Sadly, this is all at the exterior level. They do not truly have the primary principle or the substance of the trends which they are so engrossed with.

Whenever you socialize with these folks, you end up being shallow too. You begin slicing and dicing individuals based upon where they are in regards to politics, societal sensibility, principles, etc.

However, people are more than the sum of their parts. You can take someone and segment that individual to various levels, but guess what? Whenever you piece all those strata jointly, they don't amount to that individual. Something's lacking.

Perhaps we can call this the spirit. Irrespective, the reality is you can't simply dismantle people based upon these patterns and reconstruct them into a comprehensive person. You overlooked the individual.

That's just how these individuals think. They view it as level after level of things that they are able to recombine, reconfigure, and slice and dice, combine and fit. If you spend time these individuals sufficiently long, you end up being like them. Regrettably, that type of believing flops when it comes to the truth since folks, essentially, are not like that. We're worthwhile even more than the aggregate of our parts.

Toxic Personality Type # 4: The Troll

Internet trolls are frustrating. Nevertheless, the issue is they're not continuously apparent. As a matter of fact, one of the most popular sorts of trolling entails flattery. There are folks who believe 180 degrees reverse of whichever view or personal opinion you posted. They couldn't differ with you more, however, you can not tell according to their answer.

It appears like they're encouraging you. Nonetheless, what they're truly doing is trolling you since they don't agree with what you think. They're doing this for giggles. They get a twisted feeling of fulfillment in being total and complete liars. Nevertheless, the issue is that trolls at some point reprogram themselves.

It's not rare for a troll to get such a jolt getting folks to agree with matters that they themselves despise since this makes them dislike the individual or mock the person in their thoughts. Ultimately, they get so caught in their choice that they no longer recognize what the reality is. The entire extent of the game is just to get a surge or a response from people.

Rather, it's just the emotive thrill that they're receiving. "The individual is agreeing with me, and he's a total and complete moron and a dogmatist. I gotcha!" Who do you think pays the greater cost? The individual who is at least truthful with his/her viewpoint as undesirable or unpalatable as it might be, or the individual who lead him on?

Keep in mind that if you participate in this behavior, you're really selling your soul. I'm referring to your integrity. The nastiest component to all of this is that the lie ultimately permeates in and ends up being you. It enters into you. You get to a place where you don't even know which side is up. That's how puzzled trolls are.

It all comes down to nourishing insecurities since they're quite unconfident at some level or another. That's why these guys take pleasure in getting folks to claim things that they despise or say things that they deep down within wish to say.

Due to their habits, support and deceptive tactics, they get individuals to articulate out things that they wish they might say or stuff which they detest. Associating with these individuals draws out the worst in you. Furthermore, you wind up with someone who doesn't truly value you for who you are. If you're not cautious, you may wind up being like these folks. Their whole life is a lie.

Eliminating emotional clutter necessitates in your emotional habits in addition to a confirmative choice to keep away from people who have a tendency to strengthen those unfavorable mental habits. A great deal of this stuff can be fairly understandable, but it's certainly not effortless to do.

The bright side here is that you don't need to attain complete freedom from these emotional patterns and these individuals overnight. You simply have to choose to take baby steps and stick to those actions. Permit yourself to be persistent. The bright side is if you keep applying constant initiative, ultimately, you are going to become free.

Once again, please keep in mind that this doesn't imply that you need to cut out a great deal of folks from your life. You just have to place some distance between you and them so these guys do not emotionally deteriorate and taint you.

Chapter 6: Getting Rid of Emotional Clutter

Watch what you feed your mind. You need to be watching your habits and taking note of the folks you socialize with. While this is necessary, you also need to ensure that you take in the right sort of stimuli.

In any given day, we subject our own selves to all kinds of data. Surprisingly enough for the large bulk of these inputs, we are totally oblivious. There are regularly details that we notice, smell, taste, tap and listen to. Nonetheless, in spite of the countless daily stimuli we go through, we really just get to memorize a small portion of them.

Of these recollections, we only evaluate or judge an even tinier fragment. Among these recognitions, only a tiny percentage will make it to our personal story. Mostly, they either strengthen things which we currently think we understand about ourselves, or we just recall them, contemplate them, concentrate on them and ultimately lose sight of them.

Now you might be considering that this is totally ordinary. Mostly, you're correct. But the issue is that we can easily subject ourselves to all kind of stimulations which produce psychological clutter.

Now, these are separate from emotional clutter. Emotional clutter sets off your sentiments about your spot in the world, what you're about, what you can do, your connection to people, so on etc.

Psychological clutter, however, entails psychological regimens that form your personal story. How you read things generates emotional conditions. Deciding on how you opt to evaluate these stimulations takes a fair bit of effort. You need to be conscious of how your mind works.

This is where eliminating psychological clutter truly serves to help. When you police the stuff which you feed your mind with, you can recognize your psychological procedures and nullify them if they were in opposition to you.

What to be conscious of? Like I pointed out previously, we soak up all kinds of thing during the day and you need to really categorize these items utilizing broad headings in order to alert yourself about their content.

For instance, we can feed our minds superficial forms of entertainment. This could be useless YouTube videos. This could take the format of incivilities and trolling on comment sections in addition to Twitter feeds.

These are not 100% lacking value, however, they are basically useless because they're so superficial. They don't truly captivate you on any profound level. They do not challenge your presumptions about yourself, actuality and the world. Rather, they just create some kind of emotional reward. You're enjoying yourself and that's basically it.

Another form of harmful psychological input which you ought to be conscious of involves suggestions which make you less content. It's one thing to test yourself and your occurring assumptions, it's another to take in concepts which really destroy your capacity to be content. Ideas entailing your sense of value, the value of other individuals and life as a whole.

The intriguing point about this is that initially, it begins as another kind of entertainment. You could frequent certain message boards and folks only keep repeating the words "kill yourself" or saying that life doesn't actually matter or there's truly no point to anything.

There are numerous versions of this. Now I won't question the philosophical finer aspects of such ideas. Maybe on a philosophic, logical and rational grounds, there might be fire where there is smoke. Rather, I'm just planning to concentrate on their impact on you.

It's one thing to question your beliefs so you could experience your life in a more successful way. At one level or another, we certainly have to demolish any false idols which we possess entailing a mistaken belief. That's part of maturing. But there are suggestions which could make you less content since they wear down your capability to be content. I hope you see the issue here.

I'm not referring to encountering an idea which makes you examine the religion that you're born into. That's one thing. Actually, in most cases, that's healthy. I'm not promoting atheism here. Rather, I'm recommending that people really believe what they profess to believe.

In that case, whichever religion you're born with ceases being a label which is handed down from generation to generation and alternatively ends up being truly your own. You really live out the truths taught by that system of faith. You experience it play out in your life. You see that it's the truth and it's strengthened in your mind and you purposely choose it. I'm not discussing that.

I'm talking rather about concepts that damage your ability to be content. This entails the nature of humankind and the point of life. There are some ideas around that essentially result in the conclusion that it's all pointless, meaningless and hopeless.

How could you be content if you buy into that? How can you construct anything when that is the type of ideas you envelop yourself with or when you subject yourself to online material that retells that identical destructive message repeatedly?

One more kind of input which you want to be really cautious with involves harmful emotions. If you keep encountering content which just nearly always immediately places you in a negative emotional state, there's an issue. If you're sensing a remarkable amount of negativity, you are deteriorating your individual effectiveness.

A great deal of individuals attempt to deceive themselves into believing that this is just an aspect of them being real. The actuality in their minds nearly always is negative. If it isn't negative, it's a fantasy. It's some kind of self-delusion.

Well, thinking about life in black or white turns out like this. It certainly positions you for harmful emotions. You wind up rearranging your world in such a manner that your emotional pinnacles become all the more extreme.

Ultimately, you need to keep away from time wasters. Certainly, they're captivating, fun and a bunch of people discuss them, but inevitably, they just use up an excessive amount of time. This is the time you could've devoted to improving yourself. This could've been the time that you devoted to uncovering a number of truths about yourself. Opportunity costs don't just relate to economic concerns. They likewise concern your psychology.

For each second you buy in endeavors which rob you of your time, you're losing out on something more rewarding. Perhaps you could've been performing something which might allow you to end up being a more in tune, truthful, genuine individual living in integrity.

To recover from these negative psychological ideas, you have to be forthright. Don't hesitate to designate things as they are. It might appear severe, it might even appear absurd since it ends up being perfectly obvious that you're engaged in detrimental thought patterns or enabling yourself to become introduced to this content. You need to conquer your pride and simply call things how they are and simply label them.

The more you label, the more you decide to end up being mindful, the less likely you are going to keep soaking up this data and these inputs without a dispute. At least you end up being more understanding and conscious that this is happening. Ultimately, you are going to have the ability to act on them. You are going to manage to keep away from them.

Look for and Destroy Anti Affirmations

Suppose I told you that each and every day, you are performing a script in your mind? You're not very aware of this script, but if you truly focus on yourself, you're stating particular aspects of yourself, who you are, what you can do and so on. This is what psychologists call self-talk.

Now you might be assuming that this is only a basic psychological reporting system. Like you're looking out the window and you're experiencing things play out, then you're merely explaining to yourself what you're witnessing.

There's some of that, however, a bunch of it actually is some kind of reoccurring commentary regarding who you are and what you can do. You're likewise mentioning to yourself what your capabilities are.

You need to be really aware of your self-talk since if you create a damaging habit of saying bad things regarding yourself, they emerge as self-fulfilling prophecies. If you continue repeating these bad statements whenever you recall an error you performed before, what you're accomplishing is you're reprogramming yourself to become what you dread. If you keep stating that you're a moron, then guess what? You are going to become a moron.

This all results in a self-fulfilling prophecy since you are programming yourself according to the things which you keep claiming to yourself. You need to comprehend that your mind is not only kicking back and soaking up all of this passively.

It's in fact saving it and reading it as some kind of programming and don't be shocked if your damaging self-talk winds up keeping you back and pulling you down. These are anti affirmations. You very likely already understand what affirmations are. These are phrases which are meant to give you toughness and concentration.

Sadly, we also struggle with anti affirmations and in contrast to positive affirmations, we immediately take part in anti-affirmations unless we decide to be knowledgeable about them and interrupt the procedure. We're already accomplishing this.

There are 5 standard groups of negative self-talk "scripts" you have to counteract. The initial type includes self-talk which destroys your self-esteem. When you take part in this self-talk, you program yourself to feel less deserving. You continue judging yourself in the worst manner.

The second type of negative self-talk scripts consists of protection. When you state these things to yourself, you make yourself less and less self-assured, and less and less safe. You state to yourself, "You're constantly messing up. You don't actually know what you're doing. You're inept."

This is separate from "You're stupid" since when you say you're stupid, you are coming to the root of who you are. Rather, when you take part in negative self-talk which makes you unconfident, you refer to your abilities to perform particular things.

One more negative self-talk theme consists of your personal performance. You keep mentioning to yourself, "Well, that didn't work. Why should it work the following time you attempt?" You keep resaying this kind of script and soon enough, you're not even planning to make an effort.

You end up being a less successful individual because any type of skill, even though it's something that you understand like the back of your palm, will eventually deteriorate if you don't take part in it regularly and consistently. This generates a damaging descending spiral.

You get poor results, you feel even worse about it so you're less probable to make an effort to try again. There's a tight link created between lousy effectiveness, low self-esteem and lousy outcomes.

One more motif that you ought pay very close attention to consists of your absence of clarity. You could take part in self-talk which wears down your capability to appropriately see things for what they are.

Rather, you simply see things like a huge fog and it's all just involved in a perplexing label of your situation. One usual damaging self-talk script which individuals utilize is, "I'm just not fortunate."

I hope you can notice how this results in disarray because when you claim "I'm just not fortunate" you shut down all internal dialogue. There's no requirement for your logical and rational part to break down the facts of what's taking place in your life in such a manner that you are able to understand things.

If you simply dismiss all of it as simply a bad fortune, there's no additional analysis required. How could you analyze fortune? This produces confusion. This makes you intellectually idle since, believe it or not, things don't occur mostly randomly. Generally, the outcomes you receive are the impacts of your past decisions.

Regrettably, when you participate in self-talk like fortune, the system, or it's all a conspiracy, you produce confusion for yourself since you establish this rational haze that has certain aspects of rationality.

You wind up fooling yourself into believing that "That's all the research I require. I don't have to go any farther in assessing these core problems with my life. I simply need to go with the reality that I'm simply not fortunate."

Whenever you generate this confusion for yourself, you're truly robbing yourself of all the strength that you actually possess. Last time I checked, it doesn't actually make a difference what you appear like, where you originated from, where you are, the missteps you made previously, you could always decide to switch things around.

You could permit yourself to be operated by your visions and your optimism for the years to come so you could go passionately to create the sort of tomorrow you wish for yourself.

Ultimately, there's one more set of self-talk themes which make you psychologically lazy. This is, mostly, pertaining to the confusion that I pointed out prior, but it needs its own category since individuals have a tendency to soak these in.

Whenever you socialize with people, don't be shocked if you begin believing like them. This occurs since you soak up other people's perspectives and their manner of viewing the world.

You wouldn't do this if this failed to work on some level or other. Individuals are not dumb. You will just take in mental patterns only if they fulfill some kind of purpose. At some level or another, it operates, but the issue is you might be opting for an idea which is not all that profound.

It's not all that extensive and worse yet, you place yourself to live a life built upon assumptions. Rather than challenging your thinking faculties, you end up being trapped. You just search for particular signs and you begin jumping to conclusions.

Rather than permitting yourself to be sufficiently open-minded to really take a look at the facts and attempt to come up with various analyses, interpretations or even better, developing your own theory, you begin the game using this template in your hands and you're simply enforcing this template on whatever you encounter.

Not shockingly, the majority of the time, you come up with a poor match. Things which play out in your life fail to nicely match this intellectual template which you utilize. However, folks who carry this out can't be bothered.

They end up being mentally idle. If they encounter a pattern which has 5 things and 2 fit their assumptions, that will do. Be careful of the affirmations which match any of these 5 themes. If the things which you say daily result in these conclusions, then you're in trouble. Interrupt them.

Try to conquer them. One of the highly reliable ways is to just nullify them. What this indicates is that you state a different affirmation to substitute them rather than automatically kicking off into "Well I'm just not fortunate. I'm stupid." You turn things around and state another thing.

How to Create Affirmations That Actually Work as They Should

A bunch of other books make an effort to fill their pages with affirmations people can use, but allow me to tell you, they flop. Why? They do not know you.

The writers of those books clearly can't read minds. That's the reason why it does not make sense for them to come up with these canned lists of affirmations which work on individuals based upon particular circumstances. Rather, I will simply take you through a procedure of you creating your own affirmations which have a greater possibility of working. Why? They essentially match your set of conditions. They really emulate your track record and experience.

First, you want to exceed the standard and the superficial. When you offer an affirmation to yourself, you need to cut to the core of the problem. Rather of just simply stating, "I look excellent" think of the reason why being told you look excellent matters. When someone says that you look excellent, it indicates that they value you, see your worth and they feel that you matter.

Next off, you need to custom-tailor your affirmations based upon ways in which you really think. This necessitates that you hear yourself initially. When you state particular things to yourself, how do you express it? Do you simply say "I'm messing up" or "I scored big this time around" Focus on your actual inner dialogue and after that phrase the affirmation to suit that dialogue pattern.

Once again, this is one thing which only you are going to be able to discover. A bunch of affirmations out there openly fail since they appear so shallow, unnatural and basic. It is crucial to pay attention to how you really think. In what way do you phrase these subconscious words? In which way do you string them with each other? Now that you possess a fundamental idea of the affirmation you really wish to give to yourself, form and reshape these to match the method you usually use to speak to yourself. That's the way you get it to register.

Chapter 7: How to Get Rid of Clutter in Your Career

Another kind of clutter which you truly want to handle consists of what you do for a living. If you're similar to the common American, odds are you're not very delighted with your career.

The majority of folks that I've talked to in researching this book really despise what they work on for a living. If offered an opportunity, they would do something else. They could also take a pay decrease. That's how powerful their distress is with the things that they do for a living. This is a truly large source of clutter.

If you go to a job which seems like a daily degradation, what impact do you suppose that would have on the remainder of your life? A bunch of family abuse in fact develops from this. For instance, a father is miserable with his job, don't be shocked when he's not a really forgiving individual regarding his wife or kids.

The identical goes for the mom, and the youngsters. They're not thrilled with the school, which will likely produce turmoil across the board. So just how do you remove career clutter? Below are just some recommendations.

Decide to Love What You Do

The primary thing you may do is to head to work with the clear goal of loving what you do. Beginning at a particular date, I want you to purposely find the satisfaction, significance and value in what you do. Welcome it. Permit yourself to feel great about the things that you do.

Discovering the passion in what you're presently doing for a living is really simpler than you think. How am I so positive? Well, let's put it like this. In case your job is such a total and overall time waste, you most likely would have identified a reason to give up your job sooner.

If it truly burns you or if it truly is such a void in your life, you would've located the resolve and the strength to leave your job sooner. However, you're still there. I uncovered this when I worked for an insurance business and I had this buddy who walked in and he would just moan and groan about his job all the time, each day. As he was shuffling the documents, seeing the customers, looking through the handbooks and procedure books. Well, sure enough, the business underwent a reorganization and there were a number of months where supervisors, along with the management team, were actively assessing everybody in regards to firing or early retirement.

What do you presume my friends' response was? If he truly disliked this job, he would've been thrilled about the chance that he might get omitted since it includes a lovely, fat, lump sum in addition to retirement benefits. Besides, he's been working at that place for at least 20 years. However, he was terrified.

Throughout those months, it occurred to him that as frustrated as he was with regards to particular facets of his job, by enlarge, he loved his job. It was one of those substantial individual conclusions, but naturally, when he discussed this with me, he wasn't really emotionally sincere about it.

Because hey, let's admit it, if you've been griping about your job for numerous months or perhaps years to your friends and after that suddenly, you return with a total 180 degree different perspective of your work, you'd seem as a fool.

But reading between the lines, I understood what occurred. It occurred to him that his job wasn't as horrible as he believed it was. Soon enough, I began seeing him smile at the office more frequently. He didn't get retrenched, but the chance of being let go eventually woke him up to just what caused him to turn up to work for well past 20 years.

If you are in a career which you think is dead-end, drains your spirit or typically feels toxic, I wish for you to halt and consider what tasks you engage in at work which keep you returning. At the very least one task gives you sufficient passion to desire to come to work day in day out, week after week, month after month.

It might have something to do with freedom. It might have something to do with the topic you're involved with. Discover the passion in what you're undertaking. If this would not get the job done for you, the next approach which I know works features gamification. This is just a lavish word for attempting to turn particular aspects of your work into a game.

Perhaps you could look into various processes which you perform and attempt to link some kind of success at the completion of a process. Perhaps you work at an office where you can effortlessly compare your effectiveness with other individuals. In that condition, you could establish a leader board. There are really no rewards here, but by considering your job as some kind of video game, you could see yourself begin at a level and advance.

You could end up going from landmark to landmark, success to victory. It no more appears like some obscure mishmash of meaningless activities which don't truly lead you anywhere. Rather, you see a wonderful straight progression and if you handle your job as a computer game with a substantial emphasis on unlocking a growing number of achievements and acquiring more points, you could be shocked to find that your boss would like to promote you more frequently.

You may be nicely surprised by how much more cash you are going to be earning. You need to comprehend that the amount of cash you're generating at work is actually the price tag your boss or the powers which be placed on the worth of your work.

Naturally, this is marked down by their profit margin, expenses, and other variables. Still, it's an evaluation of the amount of value you bring. If you employ gamification techniques to your work tasks so you end up being more productive, your work caliber increases and you can manage harder tasks, the worth of your work improves.

For quite a long time, your boss is going to be appreciating a bargain since the overall value of your production is so much larger than the amount of cash they're compensating you.

But considering that the labor market is still a market, your boss would certainly be an ignoramus to maintain this discrepancy going for too long. Ultimately, they would begin ratcheting up your payment to get a tad closer to the genuine full value of your services.

Now don't get far too excited. It is going to by no means get there, but at the very least you are going to be earning more than you are earning now. You're not simply one more face in the crowd. You're someone who really appreciates their work. You're effectively element of that core group of workers who take things to a higher level.

One more method to utilize to love what you do is to obtain a side project. You could begin an online business, perhaps it's an online store, perhaps you may check out dropshipping. Perhaps you could even freelance on the side. No matter what the case might be, you begin doing stuff on the side which makes an income.

This has the result of guiding your attention to tasks which have nothing to do with your primary job. A great deal of the tension and negative feelings which you have regarding your job can come from the reality that you simply have all this unused time. After you come home from work, you begin considering what took place at the office and you feel horrible.

Now, rather than doing so, you begin considering your side project and doing freelance work, doing creative work or online marketing, you don't offer yourself the chance to keep mulling over things that you're distressed about.

This maintains things fresh with your primary job. Ultimately, you begin evaluating it with a different point of view. It's no longer as repressive as you formerly believed.

Discovering the Courage to Let Go

Now, as strong and helpful as loving what you do can be, for certain folks, it's truly not a possibility. They just can not discover the passion in what they're performing, gamification doesn't get the job done and try as they might, their side project doesn't keep them engrossed sufficiently.

In this scenario, you need to find the tenacity to let go of your job. It's the cause of harmful thoughts which you can't get rid of, no matter how hard you try.

You most likely prefer to look at this as your first option, but I recommend you attempt to love what you do initially. If that isn't getting the job done, you need to develop a game plan to let go.

Don't participate in the game the way the majority of other unhappy employees do. They get to a point in which the straw broke the camel's back and they put in their 2 weeks notice. Rather, set your resignation at a convenient point down the road.

Ease into it. For instance, you could state to yourself, "Okay, I'm miserable with this job. It's not actually leading me somewhere. It's creating a great deal of problems. I'm planning to quit. But I give myself 2 years or 1 year." Regardless of what the case might be, you need to give yourself a good cushion.

One useful effect of this is that you understand that at some time, your income will go down due to the fact that you will quit your job. This drives you to plan better so in this manner, whatever cash you save, you are able to invest. You could handle your resources better.

You're not placing yourself in a circumstance where the date suddenly shows up and you just need to quit and your income goes down like a rock. Then get so hopeless that you get another job which is comparable enough to the previous job which you end up being unhappy again. Your job tragedy replays itself again and again.

You need to set that date, but here's the trick. Once you establish that date, stay with it. Sadly, a lot of folks try to establish phony ultimatums to themselves. My buddy, that I detailed earlier did this constantly.

He'd frequently say to me in frustration, "In 6 months, I'm going to quit." Then he would provide me with a date and state: "Mark my words. When that date arrives, I'm out of there." Certainly, that day came and went and he's still there. He was still whining and life moved forward.

You need to establish a date when you are going to take that jump. When you do this, you force yourself to plan in advance. You begin putting away cash, building a reserve and most prominently, you begin setting yourself up for a smooth landing. Possibly you could launch an online business. Perhaps you could get a job search going which results in far better work.

No matter what the case might be, you utilize that target date to drive you to action. It's not simply like some kind of psychological or emotional bookmark. Establish a date and stay with it.

Unlocking the Power of Passive Online Income

No matter if you stick with your job or you are intending to shift to self-employment, you may wish to think about putting together a passive income online business. This includes developing an online asset that you work very hard to develop. But the bright side is you work one time, but the revenue keeps coming.

Now, don't become too excited. This does not imply that there's completely no additional work. Such systems do not exist. Regardless of all the buzz which you have heard, there's no such thing as a full "set it and forget it" money system. There's still going to be some kind of work required, but it won't occupy as much time as a full-time job.

The big distinction between a passive income and an active job entails needing to work to make money. With active income, no work indicates no income. With passive income, you may work to develop the asset, relax and still earn an income.

That's where you want to be since when you quit working on one asset, you may develop an additional asset and yet another one and before you realize it, the small trickles of online income amount to a nice stream of revenue that can not just surpass your 9-5 income, but provide you a remarkable degree of freedom.

You build them up once to get them performing and you will not need to babysit them. You do not need to do work to make money unless, naturally, you get involved in freelancing, that is actually similar to working a job but on your own conditions and schedule.

The main dynamic of freelancing is still comparable to active income. You still need to do the work for you to make money. You cease working, you don't make money. With passive income, you put in enough time once and after that, the system generates revenue by itself. If you have the ability to properly establish online passive income streams, you could lead a digital nomad lifestyle.

There are numerous bloggers around who bounce from one country to the next. They tackle many various hobbies. Their blogs generate income via advertisements. Their Instagram accounts generate income via sponsorships. You could be among those digital nomads. You should disenchant yourself of the idea that there's this set massive method to earn money on the internet. I'm sorry, but unless you are considering building a startup, that simply won't transpire and typically when you create a startup, you essentially trade your life for the business.

Startups call for a bunch of time and there's truly no proof that the startup would do well even though they can consume a lot of time, work and mental energy.

Rather, I'm referring to developing small, passive money streams and these incomes are reasonably humble. You don't actually bring in all that much, but the bright side is that when you develop a lot of them, these streams amount to a fair bit of money.

This is particularly true if you enter into e-commerce by creating your own dropshipping store. If you wish to completely own your time and delight in a remarkable amount of financial and personal freedom, explore earning from internet-based assets.

Chapter 8: How to Enjoy More with Less

There's a traditional Zen Buddhist saying "less is more" Now, for the longest time, a great deal of folks were mocking this claim. This really is regrettable since there's a bunch of truth to this. How come? Well, when I was in university, I didn't have many things. I did not have ample cash left over for a lot of food, much less, belongings. But guess what? The things which I did own, I genuinely appreciated.

I recall purchasing this nightstand from a goodwill shop. I hung on to that nightstand for near to a decade after finishing university. I really ended up being connected to it not only due to its features but likewise due to the fact that it reminded me that I don't actually require all that many things when I moved from flat to flat.

That nightstand was a concrete reminder to me that it was truly my mindset that helped to make me feel content. It's my attitude which made me believe that things were valuable and complete. I discussed this with you since it's simple to think that for you to feel safe, you need to encircle yourself with a great deal of stuff. It's easy to fall under the trap of believing that for you to feel great, the things you possess have to have the appropriate logos, labels, or have to be created by the right producers.

The truth is that these things just have meaning due to the fact that you decide for them to have meaning. The meaning stems from you. As I stated, I had a nightstand which was all shambled up and didn't truly appear all that great, but in my head, it was quite valuable. You need to embrace the same attitude with the things which you possess. Because if you read that much meaning into the items which you purchase, you wind up purchasing less.

Your mind could only hold on to so several points of reference as far as meaning is concerned. You are going to manage to take pleasure in your belongings because eventually, they remind you of what's actually genuinely valuable in your life. You no longer participate in this ineffective race of just obtaining an increasing number of stuff due to the fact that you're searching for more and more meaning.

Rather, when you decide to end up being mindful of how each single existing possession you currently have provides you meaning, you feel more content. There's less of a void in your life which you want to fulfill with people, things, ideas or endeavors.

Strip Down the Things You Enjoy

The following step you ought to take entails doing a total evaluation of all the things in your life. This consists of people, events and actual things. Carefully consider the various people in your life. What do you appreciate about them? In which way do they engage your understanding of purpose and meaning? Do the identical with the endeavors you engage in. Apply the identical evaluation to the items you own.

The more you perform this, certain trends start to surface. You begin connecting the dots and it appears that individuals, endeavors and things in your life all share particular common concepts. When you can do this, you begin looking at these factors in your life for what they are. You value them. They're no more proxies for that ultimate experience which you're searching for.

They're no longer things that you need to obtain so you may feel great about yourself. Rather, you peel all down to emotional states which are real. You begin seeing these concepts interact. Appropriately, you're less probable to keep obtaining things since, at this moment, it does not make any sense.

Uncovering the Core of Enjoyment

You may possess a ton of stuff, but do you truly enjoy it? You might have a great deal of time, but do you truly enjoy the time? These questions head to one source: enjoyment. You need to ask yourself, what could you value about your life daily? What are the things which

you truly eagerly anticipate? If you're entirely truthful with yourself, you should manage to find at the very least one things. Sadly, a bunch of individuals can't even get that far. A great deal of them are so baffled that they can't even identify one. Reflect on what you eagerly anticipate every day. What can you value every day?

Another method to respond to this question is to pay attention to loss. As the traditional saying goes, you just miss the water once the well is dry. Every day, you visit the well to obtain water. Actually, it's so standard and you've accomplished it plenty of times and now you don't even consider it. Obtaining water from the well is automatic.

Now could you picture a terrible drought and that water runs out? Before it runs out, you begin becoming conscious of how crucial it is. Before you realize it, the water is gone. You remember its value. Consider particular difficult times in your life where you lost things, people, or you were not able to participate in activities which you typically do. What can this inform you about what's significant to you? What should be essential to you? What does this reveal you about the things which you ought to be appreciating?

Fixate on the process of enjoyment. When you're appreciating something or the company of individuals or indulging in an activity, attempt to break it down into a declaration which you are able to articulate. No matter what the case might be, note down reasons why you enjoy particular items, particular activities and precisely why being around particular folks feels so nice.

After you've jotted down your responses, ask yourself, "In what way can this satisfaction improve the remainder of my life?" Simply put, if you manage to enjoy yourself in some situations, why not take things all the way? Why not discover that degree of satisfaction in other parts of your life?

Whatever You Do ... Do This

I know what I will say is simpler said than done. I know that you come with all kinds of obligations, responsibilities and duties which really necessitate your focus and you're unable to completely enjoy life and reside in the moment. I recognize that, but no matter what happens and how you do stuff, at least make an effort to do this.

Attempt to create good memories. At the moment you may be worried. You may be fighting with deadlines or other minor fires or crises occurring in your life. Even so, enjoy what you're working on since when you take a snapshot of what's taking place in your life, ultimately some of it would make it to your memory banks.

I recognize it seems like a cliché, but life is really a lot shorter than you want to admit. I know, at the moment, you're most likely trying to maintain your head above water in particular parts of your life, however, attempt to take psychological snapshots of where you are.

Make an effort to fixate on those aspects of enjoyment. Believe it or not, you are going to arrive at a point in your life from where you look lovingly back to them. Ultimately, at a particular moment in your life, you are going to understand the power of memories.

Unlocking the Power of Memories

Typically, when folks consider memories, they usually view it in practical terms. You recall stuff since it allows you to perform particular things in the future. You recall how to perform things, you remember particular days. It's designed to result in some kind of practical advantage.

Nonetheless, it's also effective in regards to your feeling of meaning and happiness. When you discover how to uncover the power of memories, you are going to have the ability to remember things willfully. It resembles watching a film from the past and as you most likely already know, whenever you see a whole lot more details in a film, you are going to manage to combine it together to a greater degree.

This has a really strong practical impact on your life. Part of the reason why a lot of us are so burnt out, afraid and miserable is the reality that we truly have defective memories. We fall short to see things in context. Remarkably, we blow things out of proportion, we concern ourselves regarding matters which have yet to occur, even though we've observed that pattern play out a lot of times prior.

The issue is memory. If you can willfully recall patterns and particulars from the past, you would certainly feel more responsible. Things won't appear as turbulent or as enormous or as insolvable as they seem at the moment. When you can willfully recall things from the past, your recollections could provide you the motivation you require to calibrate your filter.

The main reason why we have a tendency to react detrimentally now is since we have embraced poor filters at some time in the past. Whatever the case might be, we possess a poor filter. Sadly, we only uncover that it's poor when it's far too late. A greater approach would be to truly emphasize our capability to recall so our filters are clear. We immediately discover that our filters are not helping us in any way.

We organically realize that our filters are working in opposition to us rather than for us. For this to take place, you need to have the power of remembrance. You need to have unmistakable memories.

Lastly, if you were to place a bunch of focus and time on recalling your past better, this could result in mindful filtering. I trust this much is clear. All the procedures that I've explained lead to the conclusion that we are engaged writers of our reality. You need to recognize that the inputs the world is transmitting you are neutral. It is you who assigns them meaning.

We may do this passively or consciously and proactively. Nonetheless, it will take place. Sadly, a great deal of the aggravations folks have about their lives is because of the reality that they're just not aware of their individual filtering process. They only allow it to hit them. They believe that this is the reality since this is how their brain typically works. It doesn't have to result in that conclusion.

You could knowingly filter the inputs that are coming in. You could alter what you concentrate on and of these stimuli, you could alter how you decipher them. Lastly, you can transform what you decide to recall and how this connects to your personal story. That's how strong your mind is.

Unfortunately, you won't gain from this if you struggle to be aware of it and you fall short to take command of it. When you keep training your power of memory creation and recollection, ultimately, you begin filtering your reality in a really mindful way.

Chapter 9: Learn to Be Content

I wish I can say to you that there is some science to contentment. While there is a fair bit of science entailing issues focusing on contentment, in the end, it's an art. It's sort of like baking a cake. Anyone could break down the ingredients. Folks could do a great job explaining the pattern in which you mix, fold or otherwise deal with the ingredients.

But as you most likely already understand, there's a great deal more to it than that. What accounts for the distinction? Art. Art truly is all about dealing with your specific set of conditions and these conditions change as time go on. You yourself also evolve over time.

Life is an art. And naturally, one of the greatest tasks which we need to plunge into includes contentment. To end up being content, you need to care for it like an art. There's no special formula.

Rather, it's an art. And much like with every other art form, there are particular attributes which you ought to seek. Use these features. Make them get in touch with your specific individual reality and your specific circumstance for things to work out. With sufficient initiative and consistency, matters are going to fall into place.

Enough is Possible

The primary thing which you are going to find out when you look at contentment as an individual type of art is that there is something akin to enough. At the moment, you're believing the opposite. At the moment, you're experiencing all kinds of aggravations confronted with so many obstacles precisely due to the fact that you don't think that you possess enough or that you suffice.

You need to enable yourself to believe that there is a mindset of enough. In the absence of this belief, you will simply be taking chances in the obscurity. You will simply keep on struggling needlessly for an unbelievably long pace of time.

Permit yourself to strongly believe that there exists such a thing as enough. The moment you enable yourself to swear by the concept of enough, things begin to take shape. You're no more managing this confusing haze of emotions, disappointments, worries, depression, tension. Rather, you begin sealing things. You begin placing restrictions to things. You're no more shadowboxing with ambiguous ideas.

After you believe that enough exists, you at that point also need to believe that it's completely fine to stop desiring after you have attained that state of enough. This is the way in which you arrive at contentment. Sadly, there is no mystical formula which precisely takes you from point A to B.

Achieving Emotional Contentment

When you permit yourself to believe that there exists such a thing as enough, then the following step is trusting that you are able to be happy enough. Being emotionally content does not need to comply with some kind of gold standard which stays the same during your life. Rather, being really emotionally content truly hinges on your circumstances.

The circumstance will alter your interpretation of contentment, but at the very least if you're open-minded to it, you are going to have the ability to attain that especially if you need to wait for assistance to reach where you are.

The sole thing which is able to change is the way in which you choose to view your scenario and this is where emotional contentment appears. Ideally, everyone would be earning a million bucks a year, but that's not real life. We need to mentally make peace with what we possess.

At a certain level or another, we need to desire the reality that we possess. This is where emotional contentment can be found. It's a confirmative decision on your part. And it develops from the unyielding faith that there exists such a thing as enough. Typically, you think in terms of more, more, more.

Psychological Contentment

Whenever you permit yourself to feel that you have more than enough and that you are deserving enough, you are able to attain psychological contentment. It truly all comes down to your self-esteem. If you believe you're good enough and things are good enough, you need to permit yourself to halt.

This doesn't imply you need to stay there forever, but you need to rest. It's fine. Rather than draining all this mental energy attempting to assert some kind of control, you recognize that it's fine and you begin transmitting energy in a more concentrated and straightforward way.

In a way, attaining mental contentment is not a whole lot different from someone who is treading water. If you know how to swim, you realize that when you tread water, you could kick and move your legs around in a really minimal manner to remain afloat. You utilize less energy while maximizing your floating time.

Psychological contentment is a nice place to be at. You don't need to drain mental energy by returning to stuff, stressing over stuff, yanking stuff from your memory banks, distressing over them. Rather, you will have the ability to focus on the present moment and enable yourself to remain in the moment.

Spiritual Contentment.

If you discover the art of contentment, you begin evaluating your spiritual facet in a more favorable light. I don't wish to sound rough, but a bunch of modern folks frequently deal with spiritual concerns in physical means.

When you attain some degree of spiritual contentment, you make peace with the reality that there are some things in your life which you simply can not describe. You agree to them with what initially seems like an uneasy truce. Ultimately, it begins to sink in.

You begin noticing the outlines of the aspects of your life which form your spiritual hole. You could, at that point, take care of them in a more relaxed and less nerve-racking way. Everyone has a spiritual edge since essentially, this part of our self talks to our necessity for purpose and meaning.

Letting Go of Attachments

By this point, you ought to have conducted a fair bit of de-cluttering. Once that occurs, you would, at that point, be in a place to grant meaning to that absence of clutter.

This all brings about the problem of attachment. The main reason why we have a tendency to accumulate a bunch of stuff is due to the fact that we assign all kinds of meaning into them.

Ultimately, we get so adjusted to this meaning that we effectively establish an attachment to the things which theoretically create that meaning. Actually, those things are just mirrors. The meaning really originates from us.

At this point, you will zero in on this truth and take the conscious, deliberate and positive step of letting go your power of attachment.

The moment you accomplish this, you punctured deceptive assumptions concerning the source of your safety, assurance and personal pride. Now I wish I can inform you that this is really easy and simple. It seriously is not.

The difficulty is not integral or belonging to the act itself. What makes it hard is your personal attachment. The bright side is you can conquer that by straightforward dedication and decision. Keep deciding on letting go of attachment.

Initially, you may trip up, however, if you carry on, sort of like water dropping on solid rock, eventually, you are going to make a hole in that rock.
Ultimately, the solid rock is going to succumb to the water. You need to do the identical with attachment in your life.

Overcome These Enemies of Personal Change

I'm suitably aware that you're truly managing significant issues. As a matter of fact, you've grown familiar with them across the course of numerous years. The bright side is if you enable yourself to end up being accustomed to ways in which you, yourself, would resist, you could attain excellent progress.

Whenever folks attempt to make the adjustments which I explained in this book, their thoughts actually run in predictable means.

By deciding to get prepared for them and coming with a prepared response, you could go a very long way in pacifying them and getting away from their impact. But if you allow them to strike you like a ton of bricks, you might be so shocked and so unready that you return to your old behaviors.

I will just outline 3 situations here, but they ought to give you enough insight in how your brain is going to attempt to handle the adjustment which you're attempting to impose on your life.

First, don't be shocked if your brain informs you that being content indicates you're being a loser. The belief being that genuinely vibrant lives of superiority call for constant struggle, conflict, and work. Anything short of this indicates that you have missed out and you are a loser.

This is false. As a matter of fact, being really content is the sign of a winner since not only are you saving energy, however, you're concentrating energy to where it really has to move. The best way to end up being a loser is to burn yourself out by continuously chasing after your tail.

One more thing you can state to yourself is that being content indicates you are going to be abandoned. This is a deception which accentuates your need for external validation. You determine your success according to the lives of other individuals. But that's exactly the type of believing that got you into this hole from the beginning.

You're so concentrated on other individuals' expectations on you that you have forgotten what really matters to you. As a matter of fact, things might have become so bad that you are effectively living someone else's life and desires.

Being content does not imply you're getting abandoned. As a matter of fact, being content indicates you're establishing your own life's rate and you're assuming control of it for once.

Eventually, be ready for the concept that being content suggests you are decreasing your standards. This actually is only a variant of the concept that a life worth living needs to include continuous struggle.

While it holds true that to really get your life to a higher level, you need to battle against particular problems in your life. You need to confront particular challenges. But this is different from believing that you need to do this day in and day out. If you were to undertake that, at that point, your life is just one large conflict. It's simply this black hole of tension.

Contentment is the accurate reverse of reducing your standards. Since you have discovered your standards and you have determined what is deserving and meaningful, you allow yourself to become content.

Conclusion of Declutter and Organize

This book has set out how to discover to de-clutter your life on various levels. This book has likewise shown you the value of contentment. As amazing as these suggestions are, they won't do you any good if you only keep contemplating them. For them to transform your existing individual reality, you need to act on them.

Questioning how you think is a step. It's not a mental-emotional workout since it has a direct impact on how you function as well as on whatever it is you say. You need to become involved. You need to choose a date, get ready for that date and no matter what happens, begin on that date.

This likewise implies that you need to organize things right. This book has offered you a framework, however, it truly is only a sketch since you need to complete the details. Not just am I not a mind reader, I simply cannot enter your life and produce the difficult decisions which have to be made for true and successful transformation to take place. The only individual who can do that is you.

This calls for preparation and focus on details. Most importantly, this needs devotion. How crucial is devotion? Well, you really need to maintain it since real transformation doesn't transpire on a "one-time big-time" basis. It's not like you perform a bunch of activities for one week and all of a sudden, your life is significantly different.

This is not a movie. This is your life and usually, you have to make little modifications which scale up with time. This is a compounding effect in which you invest in particular activities and choices each and every day and their cumulative effect increases with time.

Having said that, for you to profit from these impacts, you need to continue performing them for a prolonged time period. Compounding, it goes without saying, is not simply a phenomenon you notice with your checking account or stocks. Rather, it also plays out in your routines. It plays out in your everyday tasks and choices. A tad of consistency goes far.

You might be feeling that you're not actually investing that much energy or you're not doing a lot of remarkable things on a daily basis. That's fine. Provided you're putting in the work, just as long as there is consistency in your activities, the outcomes is going to scale up over time.

Interior Decorating on a Budget

A Budget Friendly Guide to Creating a Home Which Makes You Truly Feel "at Home" and Happy

By Matt McKinney

Introduction to Interior Decorating on a Budget

Everybody wishes to decorate their home extravagantly, however, not everybody can afford luxurious prices. The bright side is you can construct and create a spectacular and well-designed home regardless of your budget. This guide is going to assist you produce an exceptional interior for your home that is going to ultimately end up being your sanctuary. Are you prepared to experience interior decoration without investing heaps of cash?

You landed in simply the appropriate place to find out everything you require to understand to furnish your home, regardless of your budget. Before you discover how to furnish your home, let us initially explore some misconceptions individuals have when it pertains to interior decoration. Comprehending and conquering these misconceptions, having the capability to tell the truth from fiction, is what eventually leads to success as you work to develop the home of your dreams.

Myth Buster

Interior decoration is not as tough as it might appear, however, there are individuals that might lead you to think that it is. Anybody can take pleasure in basic decorating tasks to improve the beauty of their house, whether new or refurbished. You do not need to spend a great deal of cash to produce an exceptional interior for your home. This is the primary misconception individuals believe when they consider interior decoration.

A few of the most lovely homes are decorated and designed with easy, practical and stunning things. Are you somebody that has fallen victim to this misconception? Learn precisely what is and is not true when it pertains to interior decoration, so you could develop a comfy, personal and properly designed house.

The pointers and ideas provided in this guide are appropriate for those thinking about decorating a brand-new house, or for those thinking about improving the feel and look of the home they currently have. When thinking about decorating on a minimal budget, there are particular truths you must quickly separate from fiction.

Here are some essential "truths" you ought to understand:

You could enhance the ambiance of any space in your house without spending a fortune. Interior decoration is quickly achieved even when you have little or no cash to invest. In some cases, it includes merely reorganizing the products and things in your house.

You do not need to have any experience with interior decorating to enhance the feel and look of your house. Many folks understand intuitively how to enhance the appearance of their house. I am going to teach you how to do this while dealing with a budget plan, so you could have whatever you desire, without going broke.

You can boost the worth of your house by enhancing a couple of areas of your house cheaply. You can utilize a couple of basic tools and strategies to develop a more flourishing living environment. You are going to discover this during this book.

You do need to set a budget plan when decorating, or you are going to spend excessive cash since, honestly, interior decoration is enjoyable! I am going to teach you how to set a proper budget plan later on in this book. When you produce your budget plan, adhere to it, and you are going to develop the home of your dreams.

This book is going to show you how to embellish any space in your house without spending a fortune. Whether you have $200 to invest or $10,00 to invest, you can utilize any of the suggestions in this guide to brighten the rooms in your house.

Bear in mind that the term "budget plan" suggests something different for everybody. The bright side is that this book supplies information for individuals that desire a superiorly designed interior despite their budget plan. All of the ideas, techniques and tools supplied in this guide are for individuals thinking about interior decoration without investing a fortune. There are certain ideas you could elaborate on and invest more cash on if you have the appropriate budget plan. Or, you could permit yourself to delight in the easy techniques and strategies in this book and utilize any additional cash you have on special treats for yourself or your household.

You are going to discover decorating suggestions that cost nothing, and some which might cost a couple of hundred or thousand dollars. Choose the pointers which coincide with your budget plan, and you are going to discover it simpler than you think to create the interior of your home quickly and entirely.

Are you all set to find out more? Then what are we waiting for? In the following area, you are going to take the initial essential action towards enhancing the look of your house. You are going to discover how to evaluate your house and recognize locations of your home that require the most enhancement. If you are dealing with a brand-new home, you might have to think about embellishing one room at a time.

If you intend to embellish an existing home, you could utilize the ideas laid out in the next area to identify the rooms in your home needing the most attention.

Home analysis is distinct for everybody. The actions described in the following area apply whether you reside in a duplex, little home or big compound. Ensure you read this part completely, so you can produce a plan for success when preparing to decorate the your home interio on a budget plan.

Chapter 1: Analyzing Your Home

Before you can start any task, you initially need to look at your home and assess what is crucial for you to create or revamp. If you do have a tight budget plan, you may wish to focus your efforts on a couple of living areas of your house. As soon as you have more cash to deal with, you could constantly return and decorate other spots of your home.

Certain individuals find interior decorating to be a lifelong procedure…

You might discover you spend time redecorating your home during your life. That is one reason you wish to decorate within a budget plan, so you do not wind up spending a lot throughout the procedure. When assessing your home, you ought to take an unbiased view of your home. In some cases, this includes asking someone else to go through your home with you and suggest spots that require improvement.

Eventually, you are going to choose what parts of your home to enhance. Often, nevertheless, you are going to find that working with somebody might lead to useful recommendations (like including shelving to decrease clutter). You might even discover a buddy that has experience with interior decoration. Working with a buddy when assessing your house is much less costly than working with somebody you pay to decorate or assess your home.

Common Sense Techniques

When you assess your home, you are taking stock of the things or elements of your home that you enjoy, and those you wish to alter. As you go through your home, it is necessary you use a common sense approach. Have a pen and paper nearby, and ensure you make a note of any ideas. For every room of your home you intend to decorate, you could produce different notes on different pages.

That manner in which you approach interior decorating utilizing sound judgement and useful, arranged approaches. Now, there are 2 methods to approach analysis. If you evaluate a brand-new residence, you are going to approach assessment from an "entire house" viewpoint, attempting to get the most bang for your buck. If you wish to enhance the feel and look of your present home, you can still evaluate your whole home, but might invest more time focusing on a couple of rooms in your home you know require the most attention.

The New Home Method

Evaluating your home is simple if you are working to decorate a brand-new home. Take every area separately and find what the most essential locations are for you to concentrate on. As discussed above, whether decorating for a brand-new home or for an existing one, you need to constantly approach interior decorating on a budget plan by concentrating your attention on a couple of rooms at a time.

When you purchase a brand-new home, you are going to need to evaluate what things you currently have which you can utilize in your home (such as beds or couches) and what things you have to purchase to finish your house. If, for instance, you relocate to a bigger home, you might have to purchase some extra furniture for included rooms in your home. When dealing with a budget plan, you might utilize what you have already, and decorate rooms separately, one room at a time. If you attempt to decorate simultaneously, you might discover that you invest too much cash and too much time fretting about budgeting. Take a couple of rooms, and turn them into the focus of your work.

Remodeling an Existing Home

Many folks organize their plans and schedules to decorate based upon the rooms for which they feel that they require the most assistance. Typically individuals wish to decorate a single room in the home. Others might choose a grouping of rooms, such as the bedrooms, or a single bedroom to remodel or decorate for a new arrival (such as an infant).

For certain individuals, the rooms they concentrate on are the ones individuals are most probable to see on visiting. For instance, you might wish to improve the look of your foyer or living room. Others wish to enhance the functionality of rooms, such as the kitchen area. Maybe you desire more space in your kitchen area so you may cook, but likewise entertain company. You might wish to spruce up your kitchen area so it appears bigger if you do not have sufficient counter area. Ensure that, as you walk through the rooms you wish to concentrate on, you take notes of what things are crucial for you to change.

Keep in mind, as you go through a home and begin evaluating it, you might reconsider what is important. You might wish to enhance the appearance of your bedroom, or design a brand-new bedroom for a brand-new infant entering your life. Whatever you wish to do, the secret to your success is having a budget plan. This applies whether you deal with an existing home, or whether you intend to embellish a brand-new home. The budget plan ought to be the base for all choices regarding interior decorating. Your budget plan is going to assist you choose what things you need to purchase, and what products you can decorate with little fanfare or attention. You might choose to start some

DIY tasks so you save cash and could invest cash in areas that require the most attention.

Interior decorating could be costly; however, not if you take a logical approach.

In some cases, a few of the best homes you see are those which utilize common sense decorating approaches. Common sense starts with the analysis of your home and developing a budget plan to work with. Always remember that. Never ever step away from your budget, or you might discover you plunge into debt.

Tips on Setting a Budget

You establish a budget plan by initially choosing what rooms you have to decorate. You do this when you complete evaluating your home. After you make your notes, take a seat and choose what areas of your home you wish to focus on.

If you are having a brand-new infant or have an addition to your house, this is simple. You are going to likely choose these rooms to decorate initially. If you plan to decorate numerous rooms, this could be a tad tougher but definitely possible. You are going to just have to find out how to prioritize your interior decoration, and find out how to create an interior without investing a lot.

So initially, set a budget plan. How do you do that, right?

The response is easy. Learn just how much cash you have available for decorating.

Consider when setting your budget plan your month-to-month earnings, your expenses, and just how much cash you are able to afford to invest in decorating without guilt and boosting your debt-to-income ratio. Meaning, you wish to stay away from entering into debt merely by decorating your home. So find out how much cash you need to play with. Jot this number down, due to the fact that you are going to refer back to it frequently when choosing instruments to decorate your home with.

When producing a budget plan, you might discover a couple of items you wish to charge. This is ok, simply make certain you are able to pay for those things in a short time. In case you charge excessively when decorating, you might wind up paying 10 times more for decoration than you wished to. Keep in mind all charge cards bring rates of interest. Unless you are able to pay off what you charge in a month, think hard and long prior to considering your credit balance as portion of your budget plan.

After producing a budget plan, follow these steps to assist you to evaluate your home's requirements:

Focus on the rooms you wish to decorate. Label every room. When the time comes to decorate, you are going to begin with space at the top of the list. You might halt there up until you have more cash to deal with other rooms, or move to another space if you still have a bit of extra money. You might discover, by utilizing the pointers in this book, you are able to decorate all the spaces in your house to your heart's desire. It all depends upon your budget plan, and just how much time you wish to spend on DIY projects.

Identify just how much cash you have available to utilize for interior decoration. You established your spending plan when determining your costs for the month. If you have numerous rooms to decorate, think about spliting your budget plan by the number of spaces you wish to decorate. You might then designate slightly less or more to spaces that require more assistance than others. For instance, you might wish to invest more cash when decorating the dining or living areas as opposed to the bathroom.

Make a list of the spaces you can decorate based upon your budget plan in the immediate future. Often the room you focus on as # 1 might be too pricey to decorate in the short-run. Attempt to make small modifications, and choose another top-priority room to decorate which fits within your present budget plan. If you have just one room, utilize the cash you do have to furnish the room as much as you are able to by utilizing the ideas offered in this book. Begin with high-priority things. You can constantly decorate your room additionally when you have more money.

Make certain you keep in mind items you have currently that you can refurbish to enhance the feel and look of your home, and products you have to replace or purchase brand-new (as when it comes to a brand-new room or home). Anything you can refurbish is going to most likely cost less than items you should purchase brand-new. In some cases, you need to reassess any presumptions you have regarding what interior decorating is or is not. Keep in mind, the objective here is to produce a fresh look for the rooms in your house without spending a ton of money. This might need a bit of hands-on work. You might discover you like and delight in the procedure, many people find it extremely restorative. As soon as you end up decorating your rooms, you can feel happy you contributed to creating the atmosphere you have.

When you established a budget plan, spend a bit of time time shopping around and going through the concepts in this book. If you discover you just have ample cash to work on a couple of spaces, begin your own design "savings" jar. This is absolutely nothing more than a jar you could stash a tiny amount of cash away in for a couple of months, to spare for your following decorating extravaganza. Ensure you do not take cash out of this jar. In case you feel lured to do so, then establish a closed bank account where you are punished for taking out your savings prematurely. Saving for interior decoration is just like retirement saving. You wish to stash away your cash carefully and securely, and just make use of it when the time arrives to do that without penalty.

Often, a bit of extra change is all it requires ...

Some individuals collect extra change to pay for a night out. If you wish to decorate your home, save your extra change for that. Have a piggy bank filled with coins, and you are going to discover before you know it that you have simply the correct amount of cash to spend for what you require.

Now is time to carry on to the enjoyable part. You understand what rooms you wish to embellish, you have a budget plan. Now is the time to choose what kind of individual you are, and what styles you wish your home to show. Many homes reflect the character and preferences of the owner. Make certain you spend time evaluating your own preferences, so during decorating, you choose what you are happy with.

Styles

It is essential when evaluating your home that you think about the styles which dominate your home. Learn what you enjoy about your home, and what you feel you need to change to be more "at home" in your home. If you lately purchased a house, you might discover you wish to change the whole interior. There is absolutely nothing wrong with this, simply make certain you invest ample time assessing your house and your preferences prior to making adjustments.

You do not wish to squander cash and time purchasing country-themed décor just to discover later you much prefer a more modern styled home.

Remember, when doing this, certain styles or themes might consist of more costly accessories than others, but for the most part, regardless of your style or preference, you may find methods to decorate your home even on a strict budget plan.

How do you choose a theme for your home? Consider the homes you go to and what you enjoy about them, as this is going to offer you an idea about what kind of individual you are and what designs you like the most. Think about checking out a couple of interior decoration mags so you may distinguish between modern, contemporary, country, art deco and other designs.

You must likewise inventory your furnishings and home, as they might supply some insight into your preferences and style.

For instance, do you like a modern feel and look? Are you trendy? Or maybe you prefer a more classic or vintage home. Others prefer a country appearance, while still others prefer a well balanced home styled in numerous manners.

The kinds of decorations you decorate your home with are going to ultimately reflect your character and design preferences, so this is an essential step when setting a budget.

When you pick the theme of your home, you are going to have a much better grasp of what areas of your house require the most attention when it pertains to decorating and altering the present appearance of your home. Possibly, for instance, the majority of your home has a modern appearance and design, however, you find your dining area is more contemporary or traditional. You might likewise wish to create a home which is more useful. If your home is more ornamental than you want, you may alter that. Simply make certain you understand what you desire before you begin making changes.

You may wish to alter the appearance of your dining area by including a couple of pieces or altering the furniture to show the design which encompasses the remainder of your home. You might wish to create a kitchen area which has open space and higher utility to move within.

Do not believe, nevertheless, that you need to design your home in one precise way. Some individuals choose to embellish their homes in numerous styles. Your living area, for instance, might reflect a country-like beauty, while your kitchen area might look like a country pad. While it is simpler to stick to one style, eventually, you choose what you desire (and do not want) your home to appear like. You might find it enjoyable to blend and match when decorating. This frequently works great with couples who have different preferences when it pertains to themes and styles. Work with your partner when choosing how you wish to decorate specific rooms. You could each take charge of a room so you both feel involved in the decorating procedure.

Tip

Ensure you create a list of essential things before you begin decorating. Certain things you might find you can't live without …

For some people, these might consist of couches, beds, tables and so forth. For others, essential must-haves can consist of artwork or plants. Must-haves are things which help you feel complete, but also are essential for you to feel comfy in your home.

If you have the fundamentals and just require things to complement the feel and look of your home, you are going to find decorating a breeze.

In the following part, we are going to discuss a couple of basic things you may do to enhance the atmosphere in your home without spending a bunch of cash. The entire purpose of this book is, besides, to teach you HOW to decorate without spending excessively. You are simply a step away from finding out all there is to understand …

Chapter 2: Make Small Changes Initially

If you wish to be successful at interior decorating on a budget plan, you should think small. The majority of people think that to be effective at interior decorating, they need to make remarkable changes to their whole living area. This very rarely holds true. In fact, wise decorators are those who take on tasks which are little initially, before proceeding to substantial undertakings.

In some cases, tiny changes are all that is required to make a huge difference in your home's look.

In this part, you are going to find out about certain basic steps and concepts you could take to enhance your home's look. When you take the steps detailed in this part, you might find that you can redecorate your home without investing a single cent. Odds are high you are going to invest some cash. However, you can enhance the feel and look of your house by making changes which need time, not cash.

You might find after embracing a few of the changes in this part, you need not alter your home any more. Decorating on a budget plan could be as complicated or easy as you desire. Attempt to streamline your life, and you are going to find that ending up being an effective interior decorator is the simplest job on the planet.

Here are a couple of tiny ways to make significant differences in how your home feels and looks.

Tiny Changes to Enhance Existing Rooms

1. Think about including wallpaper to a room which requires a bit of sprucing up. You could likewise utilize wall-border, which is much less costly, to decorate the upper or lower sides of a wall. At the same time, you could develop borders by stenciling or painting designs on your walls, or by getting rid of existing borders to provide a room with a new appearance or feel.

2. Locate some mirrors and put them in areas in your home where they reflect light. This is going to make the room you put the mirrors in seem bigger. Your home is going to likewise appear as if it gets more sunshine. Do not put mirrors throughout your home in locations where they detract from the room's look, or in places where they reflect unappealing things (such as your driveway or garage) unless you actually desire this.

3. Attempt restoring antiques or old furniture instead of purchasing brand-new furniture, which might be pricey, but not nearly as important as your used thing. You may do this cheaply with the aid of a neighborhood Home Depot or home improvement shop. You might have to finish and sand, then stain a cabinet, for instance, to enhance its look. In instances where you have to cover water stains, you might think about positioning a strategically positioned crocheted fabric or another ornamental thing, like a lamp.

4. Cover stains up instead of re-carpeting your home. You do not need to pay a stain removal expert to enhance the look of your carpet. A lot of individuals have spots on their carpet, and many find a method to decorate over them without investing a fortune. Let's face it. Many times, when a stain exists, it is difficult to eliminate, regardless of how much you clean it. You might wash it so that it seems to disappear, just to find it comes back a couple of weeks later on. Thankfully, no stain is impossible to conceal. And conceal it you will IF you wish to save cash. The majority of bargain interior decorators strategically utilize furniture and toss rugs to conceal hard-to-remove spots. If you have kids, purchase some affordable remnants to put over your home so you could quickly get rid of and clean them if they end up being stained.

5. Attempt allowing more light in your home. If you have curtains, get rid of them. Attempt blinds, or attempt a bare window. Simply make certain you keep your window tidy. You might wish to stencil or paint on the window utilizing paints you can discover at any hobby

shop. This produces the result of stained glass, without spending the cash. Some individuals discover they could utilize stick-on appliqués on a bare window to produce the look of stained glass. These appliqués are affordable, and you could typically discover them online. They are a fantastic tool for decorating kids' rooms, as many can be found in cartoon styles.

6. Think about including some plants or a little, economical fountain in your home to bring in a subtle atmosphere and relaxing appeal. In case you do not have a green thumb, choose something that is simple to grow, and sturdy, such as a bamboo tree (some think this even brings prosperity to luck and your home). You do not need to purchase a thousand dollar fountain. Attempt getting a little yet appealing $15 fountain online. Toss some rocks in it and let it go. You might find you feel more peaceful in your home. Fountains are additionally extremely beneficial for enhancing the atmosphere of a home office.

7. Utilize fabrics to assist enhance the feel and look of worn-out furnishings. Fabric shops sell gorgeous slipcovers and fabrics cheaply. Far more economical is it to utilize a cover or to recover an existing couch than to purchase a brand-new one. If you are not handy with a thread and needle, search for slipcovers that can immediately alter the feel and look of your couch (and even hide stains).

8. Attempt painting several of the walls in your room or in numerous areas in your home to offer your house a clean slate. You could purchase paint cheaply, and you do not need to hire an expert painter to do the work (though you could locate some college students that are handy at painting, who are probable to charge less than "expert" painters). Utilize light and brilliant colors for rooms you take pleasure in throughout the day, and soothing colors such as dark green or blue for rooms you wish to kick back in. Make certain the colors you pick match the furniture you have or the upholstery you utilize in your home. Certain individuals find excellent

painting is all they require to embellish their homes in a brand-new and significant way.

9. Try utilizing lamps without any shades, or decorate plain shades you have at home. This is going to include intensity and color to any area. You can purchase colored bulbs that include an intriguing feel and look to practically any room, and make any lamp appear terrific rather than lacking when you do not utilize a shade.

10. Utilize even more paint to make a mural on a wall or a sponge you dipped in the paint to include texture to a wall's surface. You could practice this beforehand by using the paint to a piece of old wood, or a wall you intend to repaint anyhow. There are limitless ways to decorate utilizing paint, so offer the paint a shot. Do not just consider paint as a thing to utilize as a cover for a whole wall. Consider it an accessory where possible. Some individuals, for instance, purchase low-cost stencils and furnish the walls of an area in their home by administering paint to the

stencils. This is specifically enjoyable for a kid's playroom or room, where you could stencil paint your kid's name, the letters of the alphabet or cool numbers.

Keep in mind, small changes typically make a huge impression on you and individuals visiting your home. Begin little, see what you think. If you wish to carry on, you can.

Now that you understand what it requires to alter a little room or part of your home, let us now take a bit of time to assess change on a much bigger scale. Keep in mind, even while making huge changes to the within your home, this book is all about budgeting.

Some individuals discover, nevertheless, after carrying out some tiny changes, that they change the list they created when initially prioritizing how they felt their home needs to look. In case you find the small changes you make suffice to produce a visually enticing environment, you might choose only one huge change, your "high-ticket" thing, or you might choose to stick to small changes forever, so you could decorate the whole interior of your home. Keep in mind, the choice is yours. The lesson to learn is to begin little.

Beginning small is going to additionally develop your skills and ability to make bigger changes when the time is proper. You might find you can postpone making bigger changes for a number of years when you make a couple of changes to enhance the look of your house.

Now is the time to discover how to create a huge difference in the way one space or numerous rooms in your house appear without investing a fortune. While we have actually spent a great deal of time discussing how fantastic tiny changes are (and they are), there are times when big changes are truly what you need to furnish your home.

Some refer to this procedure as the home "makeover." We have actually all seen the programs on tv, where individuals have $3,000 and need to redecorate a whole home, supplying it a brand-new, fresh face. You could do the identical thing, and spend even less cash.

Ready to discover how? Then carry on to the following chapter.

Chapter 3: Taking The Plunge

In some cases, tiny changes are insufficient to produce the remarkable changes you desire in your home. You understand this, we drilled the point into your head. Often, huge changes are likewise beneficial. You might discover after living in a house for several years, that you require a makeover. In some cases, you discover that your home requires a make-under. I am going to teach you how to carry out both, without spending excessively or too little.

There are individuals who work with budget plans which are big enough to pay for total overhauls of several rooms in the house utilizing any method they desire. If this holds true, the ideas in this part are going to aid you to decorate on a bigger scale without spending a lot. You can utilize all the cash you save for a great vacation. Keep in mind, even if doing a total makeover, there is no reason you need to spend a ton of money when decorating your house.

How do you complete a whole makeover when working on a budget plan? The response is easy ... goal setting.

Goal Setting

You already realize how essential it is for you to inventory your home prior to decorating, and how crucial it is to budget prior to decorating. When you achieve these 2 feats, you can then set goals showing your requirements and viewpoints, your desires and wants for your home.

You could establish short or long-term goals for your home. Total overhauls of your whole home are feasible, specifically when you establish short, medium and long-term goals. By carrying this out, you develop a timeline for finishing your home's interior décor.

Great Goal Setting

Great goal setting is extremely crucial for your success as a budget interior decorator. Your goals ought to reflect the modifications you wish to make and fit inside your budget plan.

Every goal you set needs to be economical, workable and achievable. Here are certain instances of great goals you could set when preparing to revamp your home:

1. Eliminate all old wallpaper in the front room within 2 weeks

2. Review colors and paints at the neighborhood home improvement shop by following Wednesday.

3. Look for discount bamboo flooring on the 23rd.

4. Re-stain and finish the exterior deck prior to the conclusion of the summer season

5. Locate throw rugs for all stains on the carpet by early Fall

6. Paint the kitchen area and great room by the end of Spring

All these goals are workable. They all consist of particular things (such as painting or getting rid of wallpaper) and a timeframe for finishing the job.

Setting goals is great when you understand you can accomplish them. The only way you have to determine whether you are successful is by assessing what progress you are making. You do this by setting times of the year or dates you wish to have particular interior decorating projects commenced or finished by.

You might discover that as you make tiny modifications to your home, your goals alter gradually, yet steadily. As you reach specific goals, you might include brand-new objectives or goals to your list.

When setting goals, attempt to prioritize your goals and line them up with the rooms you focus on for decorating or refurbishing in your home. For instance, if you plan a total overhaul of your home, yet wish to begin with the living room, your short-term goals must consist of the actions you have to take to enhance the look of this area.

As soon as you attain these goals, you may carry on to other appropriate goals. Develop brand-new ones, so the creative process never ever stops.

As soon as you have your goals in place, you may move to the following action, which is investigating the materials you are going to require to attain your goals. When examining the devices and tools you require, you want to think about the quality of the material in addition to your cost.

Normally, you can discover quality materials without paying high prices, you simply need to find out how to search for them. Many people rely on the Web when trying to find products or items to decorate their home. You are going to likewise discover that lots of neighborhood retailers and house improvement shops typically provide specials on select products throughout numerous times of the year. Have your eyes and ears open for these specials so you are able to make the most of them.

You could always look for clearance items, and stock up on them so when the time arrives to remodel, you have all you require, and you just spent the cash you planned to spend by sticking to your budget plan. Here are certain added ideas for purchasing the things you require to decorate your home on a bigger-scale, without spending way too much cash.

Purchasing Products to Decorate Your Home

If you intend to furnish your home's interior, you are going to have to purchase supplies to do this appropriately. These supplies might consist of a tool kit, wood flooring, wallpaper, glue ...

The key to an effective transition on a budget plan is organization. If you make a list of products you require to accomplish your goals one room at a time, you are going to save cash, and stay clear of paying cash for supplies you discover you do not require. You are not going to make it through if you just begin making changes without considering how to make changes wisely. Keep in mind, you need to create a blueprint for success. Set out everything you wish to alter in your home before you make any modifications, and after that, go all out.

How do you know which supplies you require? Assess the changes you wish to make to a room. If you intend to paint a room, for instance, you are going to require various supplies than if you intend to wallpaper a room. Considering that painting is among the least pricey methods to decorate, let us spend a bit of time speaking about interior painting and manners in which you may purchase low-cost paint for your home.

Painting on a Budget plan

Painting a wall or your whole home is an easy and affordable method to decorate. You do not need to paint all the areas in your home to include ambiance and beauty to your home. Actually, many people on a budget plan begin with one room, and ultimately work their way up to decorating their whole home. You might find that painting one wall makes a significant distinction in how your home appears. Attempt it, allow it to sit for a while, and after that, paint a bit more if you feel you have to.

When you choose what room or rooms you wish to paint (or which walls require paint) you should purchase appropriate tools. You do not wish to purchase unneeded items. Always try to find the ideal paint, but not the most costly. Paint is just as a bottle of fine wine. A few of the ideal wines are not the most pricey wines, but not the cheapest either.

Typically, they fall someplace in between the two extremes.

Say, for instance, you wish to paint your living room, and put a bit of artwork on the walls. To attain these goals, you might require:

A drop cloth or other product to catch paint which falls from brushes or rollers while you paint. You could purchase a formal cloth, or utilize big blankets you have no other usage for and do not mind spilling paint on as long as the paint will not leak through to the floor. Certain individuals choose coating the floors with plastic initially and after that a drop cloth of some kind. You might discover a secondhand drop cloth at a yard sales. The identical holds true of wall hangings for your freshly painted home.

Purchase indoor paint and perhaps a protective coating, to assist stop cracking or damage to your walls. In case you are unsure what kind of paint you require, ask a professional at your neighborhood interior decoration or home improvement shop. You could pick from numerous paint textures and colors. Many come with integrated lacquers or chip-proof components that are going to save you cash. Typically you are going to discover you do not have to purchase the most pricey paint to get great paint. Ask a professional to refer you to the ideal paint you are able to get within the budget plan you have. You can likewise look into the kind of paint you must purchase online. You might discover it less costly to buy paint online after talking to a professional at your local home improvement shop.

Paint brushes or rollers. Here is an additional instance of an item you wish to purchase that is of fine quality. Nevertheless, your brushes and roller do not need to be the most pricey on the marketplace.

Hooks or nails for hanging wall fixtures, unless you already have a supply readily available. You might likewise require a hammer.

A ladder if you intend to paint ceilings, or other tough-to-reach places. If you are not comfy utilizing a ladder, make certain you have somebody with you to steady the ladder as you utilize it.

Tape you could utilize to cover the borders beneath your wall so you do not mistakenly spill paint on them. You could discover the appropriate type of tape at most home improvement shops. You desire a tape that is not going to leave a sticky film on your walls, but the tape that is more powerful than scotch tape. "Painters" tape is all you need to ask for.

You might require other supplies depending upon the kind of painting you wish to do. If you intend to decorate over paint by using stencils or by utilizing the sponge painting method, you are going to require different supplies. Once again, do your research. Look for some guidance from a professional at your neighborhood paint or home-improvements shop. They are going to tell you what you require. Make certain you purchase just what you require, and not the extras they might attempt to offer you.

If you are unable to purchase all you require, learn if you have buddies or family members that might have a few of the supplies you desire, and ask to borrow them. A lot of them are going to be more than pleased to aid, and might even help you paint.

Painting Tips To Save You Money And Time

If you paint instead of hiring somebody to paint, you are going to save a great deal of cash. You do wish for your home to appear stylish, however, if you intend to paint, it is necessary you do it properly.

Here are several suggestions to guarantee you paint properly even if you have no experience painting.

-Always utilize a plastic cloth referred to as a drop cloth to shield your carpets or floors from dripping paint. I understand I've pointed this out previously, however, you would be shocked at how many individuals fail to utilize a correct cloth. You are going to spend more cash getting paint spots out of your carpet than you are going painting your walls if you are not cautious.

-Cover your paint can with plastic or place on a cardboard surface so the paint does not drip from your paint can onto your floor. You do not, besides, wish to spend additional cash purchasing items to get rid of spilled paint.

-Cover your shoes and other pieces of clothing to protect against paint spots. You could utilize basic shower caps or plastic bags to shield your shoes, and choose a worn out or damaged set of jeans and a t-shirt to utilize for painting tasks. Make certain you take the covers off your shoes prior to walking around the remainder of your house, so you do not spread out paint to floors in other areas.

-If you intend to paint the ceiling, do this initially. In case you do not, the paint may drip to your walls.

-As you are painting, constantly paint from high to low, in order to aid to avoid unneeded dripping. If you slip up, do not worry, cover it and have a go at it again.

-Tape around electrical outlets (and get rid of the covering) to prevent paint leakage. You could likewise put tape around moldings to aid to protect against unexpected spills.

-Fill in any holes in your walls unless you intend to hang a picture in the precise spot you paint over. You may do this quickly with a small "spackle" available at practically every home improvement shop. You might discover that you are able to borrow some from a neighbor or buddy, if you wish to save cash and do not wish to purchase a whole can.

-Utilize a guide when required. If, for instance, you intend to paint a dark wall light, utilize a lighter color to paint over the dark color to prepare or prime your wall, so the color you choose ends up how you want it to look.

You might wish to attempt painting a little room initially before proceeding to bigger projects. The more practice you receive, the better you are going to be at painting. Some individuals take time out of their day to follow expert painters as they do their task. You may consider this, specifically if you know somebody who paints good. Or, you might know a professional painter who might utilize a few of your services, and offer a trade, so you save cash.

For instance, you might offer to do their taxes if they paint your home interior. Simply make certain if you do go into agreements such as this, you always sign an agreement so you stay away from unneeded fights about who settled on what. You must likewise ensure you set a deadline for all work to be finished by. This aids to protect against arguments.

If you are still uncertain about what you require, check in with the professionals. Here are certain fantastic resources for information on what kinds of paints to purchase and accessories if you intend to decorate your home cheaply. By looking into these websites, you are going to save cash on a pricey consultant or professional estimate of your requirements.

Keep in mind there are countless resources you could check out regarding painting. You could even purchase books which show you how to paint well, or take classes. Lots of home improvement shops hold workshops which last anywhere from an hour to a day, and the majority of are less costly even after you purchase the paint, rather than hiring an expert painter to do the task for you.

The more time you devote to preparing, the more cash you are going to save.

Total Home Makeovers Extras

Many people wish to do more than paint when they prepare for a total makeover for their home. Thankfully, you could still accomplish this with your budget. You need to plan for these extra changes and include them into your makeover plan.

In this segment, we are going to speak about how to save cash when it comes to numerous areas of your home. You might even discover that you develop your own extraordinary ideas after reading a few of the useful suggestions and tools offered.

Many topics are covered to aid to provide the most information possible on nearly any kind of improvement you might make to your home. The suggestions offered are for individuals on any budget, however, they are going to spare cash for everybody utilizing them.

Circle the ideas or jot down the ideas you believe are going to work ideally for your home after evaluating this list. You might choose to combine a few of these with a brand-new paint task to decorate your home as you want it.

Tips for Flooring Improvement

One easy way to alter your home's look is to deal with bad flooring. Individuals with carpeted floors typically fall under 2 classifications; they do not enjoy their carpets' color or their carpets are stained and worn out.

No matter your scenario, you do not have to pay cash to have brand-new wall-to-wall carpeting set up to repair the appearance of your carpet and enhance your home's interior. You could purchase throw rugs to conceal spots on your carpet. Lots of folks place furniture over worn carpet areas.

There is this thing that you must not place carpet over carpet among some individuals. This is a misconception, so ignore it. There is no reasoning supporting this misconception. Actually, lots of home improvement shops offer specialized items to keep a throw rug from wrinkling if put atop the carpet. You might discover remnants you can likewise utilize to toss over your carpet at any carpet outlet.

If you have hardwood floors yet do not have the cash to have them refinished, think about purchasing an economical and big throw rug or more to enhance the look of your flooring. Lots of carpets are quickly laundered in a big washer, so you do not need to pay pricey dry cleaners for cleaning

In case you go to a standard store to purchase carpets or throw rugs, you are going to discover that they are really pricey. Rather, head to eBay.com or other auction websites and see if anybody is offering oriental rugs or comparable pieces such as carpet-runners, which you could put throughout your home. Search for those with minimal wear and tear. These are products you can change whenever you wish to offer your house a fresh look. You could even alter them seasonally to enhance the atmosphere in your home.

You could likewise check out ethnic or little novelty stores due to the fact that they frequently offer hand-woven rugs extremely cheaply (surprisingly). You could get a throw rug created from soft wool or comparable materials to cover nearly the whole surface of a little room for $100 in many cases.

You could likewise take a look at second-hand shops for used carpets or yard sale. One person's trash might be another's treasure. Here are a couple of additional ideas for enhancing the feel and look of your floors:

Utilize dim lighting if you wish to conceal spots or a worn carpet. Absolutely nothing makes a stain stick out more than direct exposure to the sun or intense light. Think of the lighting utilized in dressing rooms. It always makes us look our worst. Have compassion for your rugs and offer appropriate, reflective light.

Stay clear of exposing wood floors to straight sunshine or spills, as this might warp the material. In case you do spill anything on the floor, be sure to clean it right away with a dry fabric. Locate something to shade your floors if they are exposed to sunshine throughout particular times of the day.

Think about a "no shoe" rule in your house to keep your floors appearing fresher longer. Many people track in excessive dirt from outside when they wear their shoes within the home. You could have a set of slippers prepared to use in the home in case you like having your feet warm.

Concentrate on decorating other spots of your living space, and putting things up high on the walls so individuals are less probable to take a look at your flooring, and more probable to look at your tactically positioned plants, hangings or other things. For instance, you could put images throughout your home high above the flooring, so individuals instantly take a look at the pictures instead of staring at your floor. In case you have a big statue on the floor, you are going to draw attention to the floor. Once again, this is nothing more than a common sense suggestion to enhance the look of your home.

Consider snap-in "fake" hardwood flooring. Numerous home improvement shops sell DIY hardwood flooring. It might not be created from the identical material old-school flooring is. However, it could work similarly well. You could even purchase "snap-in" floor covering you actually snap into place, so you do not need to hire a pricey consultant to set your flooring up.

Remember that some flooring is cheaper than others; cork flooring for instance, and some kinds of bamboo flooring, include a lovely appearance and appeal to a home, and typically cost less than other hardwoods such as oak. They maintain the identical sturdiness and frequently last 20 or more years, so it deserves looking into. Do not purchase the most affordable items only, search for those which are durable and are going to last you a very long time. That way you do not need to stress over replacing them typically or ever, so you are going to save cash in the long-run. If you sell your home, you could include this to enhance your home's value.

Think about purchasing wood flooring which is not finished. You could stain and water seal the flooring on your own to spare cash. You could likewise ask a buddy to aid you to do this. This is another example where trading services is useful. And if you do not have a "trade" you could utilize as a bartering tool, get imaginative. Attempt offering somebody a night out, offer to look after their kids. You may discover you are amazed at how simple it is to get aid from others when you are kind, open and ready to ask.

My preferred method to improve the appearance of flooring without spending a lot is by utilizing runners in high traffic areas. Frequently you could purchase gorgeous runners, lengthy carpet stretches, really cheaply. Runners can be found in many various colors, designs and patterns. You are going to keep your floors and add to the design of your home.

Keep in mind, laminate and replica wood flooring items frequently look just as great if not better than the actual thing. They are simple to set up, and you are able to accessorize them cheaply with a couple of well-positioned throw rugs. These are an outstanding option for individuals that wish to improve their home interior without spending a lot on carpets.

Accessorizing Rooms with Hangings, lamps and More

Yet another method to decorate your home elegantly without spending a ton of money is to accessorize. The majority of people over-accessorize. If you wish to budget, search for a little selection of quality pieces and if anything, think about under-accessorizing your home. A couple of unique pieces well positioned in your home are going to prove a lot more intriguing than a house loaded with numerous inexpensive accessories.

Accessories consist of lamps, wall hangings, paintings, vases, plants and other things that can bring a sense of elegance and peace to an area or your home. You could likewise include things you create, including paintings, dream catchers or items your kids make at school (hang their artwork on the walls). Keep in mind, you wish to develop a home which offers appeal, yet one that likewise reflects your character. Put what you like out, and put your accessories in handy, attractive places.

You could likewise create a special appeal by choosing one recognized item and utilizing it as the focal point for the room you decorate. Simplicity is crucial if you intend to include a unique object in your home.

Let's say, for instance, you wish to decorate your dining area. You initially repaint the walls in a stylish color. You then have a dining room table purposefully positioned in the middle of the room. Pick one classy item as the focal point for your dining area. This might be a vase, for instance, which you fill with fresh flowers.

The tinted walls and focal point will be the things which stick out.

Suggestion For Dealing With Clutter

In some cases, the ideal way to enhance the look of your home and enable room for "decor" is to eliminate clutter. You can quickly acknowledge a clutter bug. They have stacks of paper piled atop the fridge.

Drawers filled with needless. Knickknacks throughout your home ... the list goes on. Rather than worrying, why not construct or purchase an affordable cabinet, one which is visually pleasing, and "keep" your clutter there?

This is an easy way to conceal clutter, which constantly makes an area or home appear 10 times better. Ultimately, if you have time, think about getting rid of as much clutter as you are able to. Some individuals stack their clutter in their garage. What takes place if you relocate to a little place? Attempt setting aside a day every month to look through and get rid of the clutter you have in your home. You are going to discover that you feel invigorated for doing so, and enhance your home's utility and look.

In case you have cabinets, you could always have them shined and refinished to aid them to look their finest, or perhaps add low-cost handles to enhance the feel and look of your cabinets. The majority of people instantly presume they need to switch out something that looks used. Extremely rarely is this the case. In fact, worn items which get a little TLC typically lend an extra appeal to a room since they are charming.

Keep in mind, when making over a home, typically less is more. It is the little details and the individual touches that individuals frequently notice. You can alter the lights in your home to incorporate beauty. You could change the fixtures on a used faucet to make it appear fresh. These little changes do not cost much, yet could make a huge difference.

The Main Three Changes Everybody Can Make

In this part, you are going to discover how 3 basic changes can change how you feel about your home in a single second. You could decorate your home quickly if you embrace even one of these concepts. You could utilize these changes to decorate an area or a whole home, even if they just have a little budget plan to deal with.

Initially, always buy the paint. Keep in mind, paint is the interior decorator's best buddy. You could utilize paint in numerous ways to enhance how your home looks.

Next, think about getting rid of clutter. You could actually remodel your whole home simply by getting rid of clutter. You might find it surprising simply just how much an uncluttered area means.

Last, include a couple of crucial pieces, such as the artwork you purchase at an auction, at a yard sale, or that you create yourself, to decorate an area or your home. Think about, for instance, family photos. You could sort through photos and make collages of members of the family to decorate your walls.

You could purchase low-cost wood frames and paint them to produce a distinct wall hanging for any area in your home. When it pertains to budget plan interior decorating, even when attempting to makeover your whole home, in some cases, basic changes are the ideal changes to make. One technique lots of people find extremely useful when interior decorating on a budget plan is Feng Shui. In the following part of this book, you are going to discover more about this ancient practice. Learn how to place it to use and save cash when decorating your house's interior, no matter the design or theme you pick for your home or living area.

Feng Shui On A Budget

Among the more prominent methods to decorate the interior of home nowadays is a method called Feng Shui. You could work with a pricey Feng Shui professional to decorate your house, or utilize the basic tools laid out within this book to create a well-decorated and tranquil home.

Feng Shui is not a mystical and magical system. It is an ancient, practical art meant to assist individuals in creating their living space in such a way which promotes positive energy and recovery. There are numerous easy principles you are able to embrace when decorating your home that are going to enhance the look of your home, and perhaps your health, luck wealth and success while at it.

The objective of Feng Shui consists of making a living space which is well balanced. Generally, homes decorated properly are well balanced, well designed and clutter-free. They are appealing on numerous levels to many individuals, which is why I chose to devote a whole chapter to the art of Feng Shui. Some essential factors to consider in Feng Shui consist of color, which lots of people believe has an impact on emotion, and "flow" or the balance of good energy.

You are going to find out more about each of these essential elements in the sections ahead.

Feng Shui and Color On A Budget Plan

Painting your walls is one method of decorating your home. The colors you pick can have an incredible effect on how you feel while in your home. Many individuals, including researchers, think color impacts individuals in various ways. If you wish to enhance how you feel AND embellish your home, you need to paint, but you likewise need to paint utilizing the appropriate colors. You want the colors you choose to bring out favorable feelings and emotions to generate balance.

How do you do that? You consider how color impacts your character, your spirit, and your dislike or like of a space or place in your home.

Some individuals, for instance, react to dark colors as relaxing and cool, while others find them anxiety-inducing or gloomy. It is necessary you acknowledge the common reactions related to numerous colors and discover how YOU respond to color prior to painting a room or area in your home.

Have you ever walked into a location where you felt really calm? Did you see the colors in the place? Begin taking notice of color as you go through your everyday activities. You might begin to see some colors trigger favorable reactions in you and others.

Lots of feel blue and green, for instance, are unwinding colors. Red frequently stimulates individuals, however, this is not always the case. Certain individuals feel the most calm when surrounded by deep, abundant colors.

Many individuals find intense colors annoying, so have this in mind when painting your home. Your home is going to be the location where you discover the greatest serenity, however, you are going to likely, likewise, welcome others into your home. The color in your room might establish the tone for your engagements and interactions with others.

Many folks find darker rooms tiring or depressing. This could be helpful if you wish to induce sleepiness, however, it is not good if you wish to prevent people from feeling sad.

Does this suggest all dark colors are bad? No. You need to determine what colors you like and what colors you need to stay away from when decorating. After doing this, you could paint freely, understanding you are creating a space you can genuinely call home.

Prominent Colors

If you have an interest in home decorating utilizing color, here are certain prominent color choices and their meanings. You could choose to paint your whole home a uniform color, or paint area by area.

Bear in mind that subtle distinctions in color might have a profound impact on how you respond to color, so make sure you "test-drive" a color prior to painting your walls.

You could do this by going to a neighborhood home improvement shop and getting a couple of swatches of color. Additionally, you can purchase a little color can you believe you want and paint a little area, or one wall, and see how you respond to it.

-Red-- if you wish to develop an enthusiastic environment, one loaded with energy, heat or power, red could be an excellent color. Many individuals alternate shades of red or red colors with abundant cream colors when painting their bedrooms. Bear in mind, nevertheless, for some red additionally inspires sensations of irritation or hostility, so make sure to determine your reaction prior to painting.

-Yellow-- this color normally inspires happiness, joy, favorable feelings, a feeling of freshness or clean, hope, and reminds individuals of the sunlight. Yellow can likewise imply something harmful or dangerous to some individuals. You might think about a pale shade to counter this impact.

-Blue-- this is an outstanding color to bring peace and serenity into any room in your house. It might likewise work as a hunger suppressant, so you may consider it for your kitchen area if you wish to stay in shape and trim. Certain individuals find darker blue tones depressing.

-Orange-- this color, such as yellow, is loaded with vibrancy and energy. It is an excellent color if you desire a productive and lively home.

-Green-- this is likewise a nurturing color and many find it calming. Some think it brings good fortune and for others, it signifies a more natural environment or nature. Nevertheless, green can likewise signify "envy" or jealousy, so track your sensations around this color.

-White-- there are numerous white shades. If you choose pure white, you might inspire sensations of purity, or you might inspire a hospital or clinical environment, so be weary of the shade of white you utilize. Lots of people find that white color signifying inner peace and a feeling of humbleness. In certain cultures, white represents death. Think about the white lily, a stunning white flower typically used throughout funerals. Be weary of your beliefs and response regarding this color when decorating.

Encertain you test drive these colors. Take a look at the colors above. Spend a bit of time with every color. Purchase fabrics of these colors and choose which colors you take pleasure in the most, and what energy they supply you with.

This is going to assist you when you choose colors to paint the areas of your home.

Positioning of Objects in the Home

How you position or where you position items in your room impacts your environment. The majority of people think it is ideal to create open spaces where you are able to walk freely.

More than once, we discussed how essential it is to get rid of clutter when you can. In Feng Shui, the objective of putting things is to promote the motion of energy, referred to as "chi" in any room. This brings favorable sensations and prosperity.

Here are certain simple actions you could take to create a reasonable, functional and beneficial circulation in your living space:

Ensure all walkways are roomy, and open so you feel you have more area and do not trip on things.

Do not obstruct doors, and make sure they can open easily to enable heat and success into your home.

Avoid clutter in any part of the home as this could generate sensations of mayhem or a disorganized environment. It could likewise obstruct favorable energy.

Attempt to permit air to stream easily through rooms, utilizing ventilation or by uncovering or unclogging windows.

Avoid putting a bed straight across from a door or mirror as this can disrupt your natural sleep cycle or rhythms according to some.

Make certain mirrors reflect favorable or visually enticing things, so when you look at them you feel relaxed and tranquil.

Utilize plants to design an environment loaded with animation and life, and to supply a feeling of calm when operating in a stressful environment.

Feng Shui is frequently extremely methodical in its nature. Individuals study Feng Shui for several years prior to mastering the art of developing a favorable and energetically balanced environment. Simply bear in mind, your goal is to develop an area YOU feel comfy in. You might find putting your couch on one side of a room, for instance, brings you more happiness than putting it on another.

Constantly utilize your instinct when putting things throughout your home, and odds are you are going to develop your home pleasingly. You might find you put items and move them often up until you develop a comfy workplace. This is completely normal. You might likewise discover with time that you have a requirement to alter the way things are put in your home. Do what you feel is appropriate at the time, and you can't fail.

Some state when it pertains to Feng Shui, it is ideal to make tiny adjustments initially, so you are able to observe how your body responds.

If for instance, you paint a room, move your couch and put a brand-new fountain in a corner on the identical day, and feel different, how could you be certain if all or one of these caused your sensations?

When decorating and moving things around to enhance the circulation of energy, make certain you take the time. This is the ideal method to generate a peaceful and tranquil environment. If you want, reorganize the furnishings in your home and walkways numerous times, to make certain the interior shows your real character, desires and wishes.

If you wish to find out more about developing a favorable and roomy environment, have a look at a couple of books on Feng Shui from the library. You could likewise Google the term and discover a plethora of information on the internet.

Professional Design Tips

Now that you have a fundamental understanding of what style is all about, it is time to evaluate some methods to bring your home together. You must constantly work to create a house that appears balanced. You do not wish to decorate your home so that you feel you reside in a disorderly environment. You could quickly decorate and produce a favorable balance by following the methods laid out in this part.

You know you can purchase affordable pieces to furnish your home. You can likewise blend and match. One secret to developing a pleasant environment is to purchase a couple of essential pieces you like, even if they are costly, and complement the remainder of the area you intend to decorate with basic items which cost a lot less.

Blending and matching work well as long as you have some style aspects in mind. For instance, if you wish to blend antique furnishings with some modern pieces, you can do so, simply ensure the pieces match each other somehow or match the general design you wish to generate within your home.

Decorating for Success

If you take a look at interior design, there are 2 major methods to decorate. You could keep things tidy, straightforward and structured (as one may if they wished to utilize the concepts of Feng Shui), or you could make a natural, positive and abstract environment which fits your character.

Some individuals choose to utilize exotic or enjoyable pieces throughout their houses to develop an amusing and dynamic environment. Others wish to develop a tranquil and peaceful environment. Still, others purchase pieces showing their cultural heritage. No single method is the proper way, since everybody is different. How you decorate should reflect who you are and how you feel.

You might discover you want an exotic style or design in the family area or the bedroom, yet serene and well balanced in the living or home office area.

You could blend and match, though the majority of people have a tendency to stick to one style or another. The secret to your success is your capability to have an open mind, and have a good time.

Make certain you do not utilize a lot of pieces when designing. In case you have a plan to place family photos along a corridor, for instance, as a method to embellish your walls, do so, however, do it simply. Attempt utilizing the identical frame design for all the pictures you utilize. If you blend and match a lot of various designs, you are going to create a disorderly looking environment.

Candles Décor

Some individuals decorate with color and candles alone. Candles can be found in lots of sizes, shapes, colors and aromas. You can purchase little tea candles for less than a buck, or bigger candles for 10. You could utilize candles to accessorize or candle lamps to replace artificial lighting in your house. If you desire an eco-friendly home, you might wish to purchase organic candles.

The trick to making candles work is discovering appropriate holders. These you can discover anywhere. You could purchase sets of candleholders and utilize them to decorate a whole home, and save cash by buying more instead of less.

Simply ensure if you intend to light candles, you substitute them routinely. Tea candles are ideally utilized as lighting sources due to the fact that they are affordable. You do not wish to purchase a $200 ornamental candle and light it, needing to replace it month-to-month. That gets costly.

On the other hand, you could utilize the bigger piece as décor, and light tea candles to enable a pleasing radiance and aroma. Many people discover a mix of methods creates simply the appropriate feel and look for their home. One word of warning - If you do purchase candles, make certain you buy candles which have safeguards. You do not wish to burn down your wonderfully decorated home. Always ensure you extinguish candles when you are finished with utilizing them.

If you are sensitive to scent, attempt utilizing unscented candles. Numerous candles come in powerful scents, so make certain you examine the candle's components BEFORE you purchase, so you do not cause an allergy when decorating your house.

As you continue to utilize your creativity and embrace brand-new methods, you are going to discover new ideas that motivate you to alter the feel and look of your home. When this occurs, return to your goal-setting list and develop brand-new goals for your house. Eventually, this is going to enable you to develop a skillfully created home whenever you desire, without investing a fortune.

I hope that you enjoyed reading through this book and that you have found it useful. If you want to share your thoughts on this book, you can do so by leaving a review on the Amazon page. Have a great rest of the day.

Printed in Great Britain
by Amazon